Simply ...

Deb...

Fruit and Vegetable Recipes
from
The Lost Gardens of
HELIGAN

Heligan Gardens Limited
for
The Heligan Trading Co.

There are too many of you to mention, but thanks to all those at Heligan who nobly and uncomplainingly consumed endless servings of recipe samples at all hours during the day and night, and thanks for all your valuable suggestions.

First published in Great Britain 1995
by Heligan Gardens Ltd for The Heligan Trading Co,
Pentewan, St Austell, Cornwall PL26 6EN, England.

ISBN 1 900270 00 5

Illustrations by Zowie Keating
Designed and produced by Production Line, Oxford
Printed in Great Britain by Redwood Press, Trowbridge

Contents

Introduction 5
Vegetable Garden Soups 9
Summerhouse Salads 19
Vegetable Side-Plates 27
Hearty Main Dishes 59
Just Add a Little (Purées and Sauces) 69
Desserts, Pies, Puddings and Cakes 75
Notes for Recipes 107

Heligan Vegetables (with recipe references)

Asparagus 109
Aubergine 109
Beetroot 110
Leaf Beet 110
French Bean and Runner Bean 111
Broad Bean 111
Broccoli 112
Brussels Sprouts 112
Cabbage 113
Cardoon 113
Carrot 114
Cauliflower 114
Celeriac 115
Celery 115
Chicory 116
Courgette 116
Cucumber 117
Fennel, Sweet 117
Garlic 118
Globe Artichoke 118
Jerusalem Artichoke 119
Kale (Borecole) 119
Kohlrabi 120

Leek 120
Lettuce 121
Marrow 121
Mushroom 122
Onion 122
Parsnip 123
Pea 123
Pepper 124
Potato 124
Pumpkin and Squash 125
Radish 126
Scorzonera and Salsify 126
Shallot 127
Spinach 127
Spring Onion 128
Swede 128
Tomato 128
Turnip 129

Heligan Fruit (with recipe references)

Apple 131
Apricot 132
Banana 132
Blackberry 133
Currant, Red and White 133
Fig 134
Gooseberry 134
Grape 135
Lemon 135
Melon 136
Nectarine 136
Orange 137
Peach 137
Pear 138
Pineapple 138
Plum 139
Raspberry 140
Rhubarb 140
Strawberry 141

Conversions 143

Introduction

One of the great Anglo Saxon cultural traditions, handed down painstakingly from generation to generation, is to turn wonderful natural ingredients into appalling food. This took a long time to achieve, but after years of practise, a method was perfected for eradicating not only all flavour, but almost all nutritional value from vegetables and fruit, skilfully achieving a universal texture so unpleasant that we are cunningly convinced that it must be doing us some good.

Academics have speculated that in Britain the root of the problem stems from the early immersion of children into a system of education where the consumption of terrible food is regarded as both an important rite of passage as well as a bonding ritual. Thereafter, those who have gone through this mill will forever find bad food consoling, in much the same way that certain men find women who remind them of matron, irresistible. The other rather unexpected outcome of this training is that the eating of good food is regarded as being something rather naughty, but nice. The almost erotic way with which the British discuss the pleasures of the palate is not displayed anywhere else in the world that I know of. This education system, when married to British reserve and the desire never to make a fuss, means that there will never be any possibility of standards being raised except by a dedicated band of fifth columnists infiltrating the system!

Joking apart, it is very worrying that recently released statistics from America reveal that eighty per cent of Americans under the age of thirty-five cannot cook. This statistic is probably mirrored in Britain where the pre-packed food industry aims its marketing at a susceptible public by creating 'easy cook' ranges that imply in their very message that cooking is difficult. Of course, we know it isn't. When Laurence Hills started The Henry Doubleday Research Association, which looked into organic horticulture and heritage seed preservation, he was struck by the fact that the longevity of gardeners exceeded that of any other profession, and he put this down to the eating of fresh vegetables. Subsequent evidence from around the world indicates that those who have a high vegetable and fruit diet are statistically far less likely to get a range of cancers and heart problems. We have always known that 'we are what we eat', so it is odd that we are surprised when we find evidence to prove it! Have people really forgotten, or simply never learned, that nourishing food is natural food - the more nourishing if it is eaten fresh from the garden and carefully prepared?

The Lost Gardens of Heligan, near Mevagissey in south Cornwall, are the site of the largest garden restoration project in Europe. Buried under mountains of ivy, bramble and rampant laurel for more than seventy years, this superb collection of walled and productive gardens, within the pleasure grounds, was a time capsule that enabled us to restore the garden as a 'living museum', celebrating the skills and talents of the ordinary men and women who made such gardens great. It was in places such as this that the Head Gardener held sway and brought his talents for 'forcing', 'retarding' and 'keeping' to bear, providing fresh fruit and vegetables for the table, season by season, throughout the year. Up until the First World War, such gardens were commonplace, ranging from the small vicarage walled garden at one end of the scale, right up to the enormous estates at Frogmore, Chatsworth and Tatton Park at the other.

The real tragedy lies in the fact that this element of our heritage has been so sadly neglected that it has now all but disappeared, save for those few working gardens dedicated to the preservation of its traditions. Heligan is the jewel in this crown, for only here can the public see the old techniques practised and varieties grown, demonstrating the richness of this forgotten era.

Here, for the first time in more than a hundred years, you can see the manure-heated pineapple pits lined with tan bark, producing fresh pineapples for the high table; the cucumber and melon house groaning under the weight of its produce; the giant glasshouses returned to their historic use with their crops of grapes, peaches and citrus. The forcing pots lining the kitchen garden blanching the rhubarb, sea kale and chicory are not mere relics of a bygone era, but an essential tool of contemporary husbandry with its roots linked to the past. The dark house, cold frames, potting sheds, root and fruit stores complete the picture of an integrated self-sufficient working garden.

The full story of the restoration at Heligan can be found elsewhere, but part of the work concerns the pursuit of fruit and vegetables expressly grown for flavour. We have set ourselves the task of establishing which varieties have all but vanished over time due to the commercial growers' demands for high yield, ease of transport, storage capability, synchronised ripening and disease resistance - all too often, flavour was the sacrifice. Using organic growing methods and a large labour force, we have reintroduced these disappearing varieties with the prime condition that they possess this quality of flavour. It was during the course of our sampling that we decided to embark on the creation of a recipe book to complement the research of our garden staff. The challenge was for us to bring flavours from the garden to the dining table with as much care as the gardeners have taken in nurturing these flavours from the earth. The real joy is undoubtedly to make a selection of menus for each season, based upon the availability of fresh produce which naturally coincides with what we feel like eating. What greater treats are there than the first tender tips of asparagus in spring-time; fine juicy strawberries for a midsummer's day; or the warmth and comfort of a thick soup at the darkest end of the year? The colours and perfumes of each trigger a chain of symbolic associations at the core of our identity and sense of well-being.

Every single recipe contained within these pages has been tried and tasted here by the staff at Heligan – only those which won almost unanimous approval have been selected. All the recipes are simple, easy to follow and often quick to prepare, providing plenty of inspiration for your own creative impulses. We hope you will enjoy them as much as we have.

HAPPY EATING

Tim Smit

Vegetable Garden Soups

Cream of Broccoli Soup

A wonderfully delicious soup which can be a meal on its own, served with some crispy country bread, freshly baked or heated in the oven before serving. The quantity of milk may be varied according to how thick and creamy you like your soup.

Serves 4-6
150g (5oz) onion, chopped, (1 medium)
400g (13oz) broccoli, chopped
2 cloves garlic, finely chopped
1 medium sweet green pepper, chopped
30g (1oz) butter
1 bay leaf
½ teaspoon dried basil
a pinch of dried thyme
1 teaspoon cumin seeds
½ teaspoon mustard seeds
2 teaspoons fresh ginger root, finely chopped
black pepper to taste, freshly ground
600ml (1pint) water
240ml (8fl.oz) milk, lowfat if preferred
120ml (4fl.oz) sour cream

1. Melt the butter in a large frying pan. Add the onion and bay leaf, sauté over low heat until the onion is soft and translucent. Add the ginger and garlic, cook for 3 more minutes, stirring constantly.

2. Add the green pepper, broccoli and water to the frying pan. Cover the pan and simmer over medium heat until the broccoli is very tender, about 10 minutes.

3. Add the remainder of the herbs and spices to the frying pan and simmer covered for another 5 minutes.

4. Remove the bay leaf, place the ingredients in the blender and purée with the milk until the consistency you require is reached.

5. Return to the pan and heat gently. Whisk in the sour cream and serve hot.

Carrot Soup with Ginger

This is a surprisingly sweet, yet spicy soup with a lovely thick texture which may be diluted with extra milk if you prefer.

Serves 6
1kg (2lb) carrots, thickly sliced
1 medium onion, chopped
2 cloves garlic, finely chopped
2 tablespoons fresh ginger root, finely chopped
15g (1/2 oz) butter
1litre (33fl.oz) water
1/4 teaspoon cumin, ground
1/4 teaspoon fennel seeds
1/4 teaspoon cinnamon, ground
1/4 teaspoon dried mint
1/4 teaspoon coriander, ground
90ml (3fl.oz) milk, lowfat if preferred
3 tablespoons lemon juice
125g (4oz) lightly roasted cashews, chopped

1. Scrub and trim the carrots. Cut them into large pieces and place in a large saucepan with the water. Cover, bring to the boil and simmer until very tender, 10 to 15 minutes.

2. Melt the butter in a small frying pan and add the onion, sautéing over low heat until soft, about 5 minutes. Add the garlic, ginger, mint and spices and continue to cook, stirring well until all the ingredients are well mixed and the onion becomes soft, about 10 minutes. Add the lemon juice.

3. Put the carrots (with their cooking water), milk, sautéed mixture and roasted cashews into the blender. Purée until smooth, adding extra milk according to the consistency you require.

4. Return to the pan and heat gently until ready to serve hot.

Celery and Sunflower Seed Soup

A lovely creamy and textured soup.

Serves 4-6
250g (8oz) celery, sliced finely
1 onion, finely chopped
1 tablespoon butter
1 tablespoon sunflower oil
125g (4oz) sunflower seeds
150ml (5fl.oz) milk, lowfat if preferred
750ml (25fl.oz) vegetable stock
150ml (5fl.oz) natural yoghurt, lowfat if preferred
1 teaspoon dill seeds
1 bay leaf
black pepper to taste, freshly ground

1. Heat the oil and butter in a small frying pan. Add the onion and sauté until translucent, about 5 minutes, stirring constantly.

2. Meanwhile, place the sunflower seeds in a dry frying pan, or under the grill and toast for a few minutes until slightly golden. Trim the stem ends of the celery, pulling away any strings, then slice the stems finely.

3. Transfer the onion and cooking juices to a large saucepan, add the celery and toasted sunflower seeds. Pour in the vegetable stock and the herbs, stirring well.

4. Bring this mix to the boil, then simmer gently uncovered until the celery is tender, 20-30 minutes. Stir occasionally while cooking.

5. Once cooked, cool the soup slightly and remove the bay leaf. Transfer to a blender, add the milk and blend until quite smooth. Season with the pepper.

6. Return to the pan, add the yoghurt and reheat gently. Serve immediately when hot.

Fennel Soup with Potato

A simple, yet sophisticated soup in which the delicate aniseed-like flavour of fennel combines with the potato in a wonderfully subtle way. (Will freeze well for days).

Serves 4-6
1 small fennel bulb, finely chopped
some fennel leaves, finely chopped
4 medium potatoes, thinly sliced but not peeled
4 small onions, thinly sliced
15g (1/2 oz) butter
1/2 teaspoon caraway seeds
1/2 teaspoon fennel seeds
1/2 teaspoon white pepper, ground
1litre (33fl.oz) water

1. Melt the butter in a small frying pan, add the onions and cook over low heat until the onions are extremely soft, about 15 minutes. Stir frequently.

2. Transfer the cooked onions to a large saucepan. Add the potatoes, fennel bulb, caraway and fennel seeds. Add water and bring to the boil. Cover and simmer until the potatoes are soft, 10 to 15 minutes.

3. Purée in a blender until a fairly smooth, yet thick consistency is reached.

4. Return to the pan and reheat gently. Mix in the white pepper and serve hot with the chopped fennel leaves as a garnish in individual bowls.

Cream of Jerusalem Artichoke Soup
The Head Gardener's Favourite

A wonderfully creamy and wholesome soup, with a lovely delicate flavour.

Serves 6
1kg (2lb) Jerusalem artichokes, sliced
2 medium onions, sliced
4 cloves garlic, chopped
60g (2oz) butter
450ml (15fl.oz) milk, lowfat if preferred
240ml (8fl.oz) single cream
600ml (1pint) vegetable stock
black pepper to taste, freshly ground
$^1/_8$ teaspoon ground cardamom
30g (1oz) flaked almonds, toasted

1. Melt the butter in a small frying pan, add the onions and sauté gently for 5 minutes. Add the garlic and cook another 3 minutes, stirring constantly.

2. Transfer this mix into a large saucepan. Peel and slice the Jerusalem artichokes and add these to the saucepan. Mix in the vegetable stock, cover the pan and simmer over low heat until the artichokes are tender, 15 to 20 minutes.

3. Once cooked, leave to cool slightly. Put the cooked artichokes into a blender, add the black pepper. Purée until smooth, then return to the pan.

4. Reheat gently on low heat, stirring in the milk, cream and cardamom. Be careful not to boil but heat while stirring constantly.

5. Serve hot with a sprinkle of almonds in each bowl.

Parsnip and Potato Soup

A quick and easy soup to make with plenty of spicy flavouring.

Serves 4-6
250g (8oz) parsnips, sliced but not peeled
250g (8oz) potatoes, sliced but not peeled
1 clove garlic, finely chopped
1 onion, sliced
1 tablespoon olive oil
600ml (1pint) vegetable stock
1/2 teaspoon ground cinnamon
1/2 teaspoon ground ginger
1/2 teaspoon turmeric
2-3 tablespoons wholegrain mustard
boiling water
60g (2oz) extra mature cheddar cheese, grated
black pepper to taste, freshly ground

1. Place the sliced parsnips and potatoes into a large saucepan of cold water. Bring to the boil and simmer until tender, 10 to 15 minutes. Drain.

2. Heat the olive oil on low heat in a small frying pan, add the onions and sauté for 5 minutes. Add the garlic and cook another 3 minutes, stirring constantly. Add the cooked parsnip and potatoes and fry for 5 minutes, constantly turning. Leave to cool slightly.

3. Put the sautéed mixture into a blender with the vegetable stock, cinnamon, ginger and turmeric. Blend until smooth.

4. Return to the saucepan and reheat through.

5. Serve immediately while hot. In individual bowls, stir in 1 teaspoon wholegrain mustard and a handful of grated cheese just prior to serving.

Jen's Spicy Pumpkin Soup

This is a deliciously rich, heart-warming soup. Serve as a meal on its own, with some freshly baked crunchy home-made bread.

Serves 4-6
500g (1lb) pumpkin, any type, chopped
1 medium onion, finely chopped
1/3 teaspoon cumin seeds
1/4 teaspoon nutmeg powder
a pinch of chilli powder
juice of 1/2 lemon
1.2 litres (2 pints) vegetable stock
black pepper to taste, freshly ground
2 tablespoons fresh chives, finely chopped
4-6 tablespoons natural yoghurt, lowfat if preferred

1. Peel and remove all the seeds and fibrous pulp, then chop the pumpkin into chunks. Put the vegetable stock into a large saucepan, add all the ingredients (including the pumpkin), except the chives and yoghurt. If necessary, top up with some extra water.

2. Bring everything to the boil, then simmer uncovered until the pumpkin is soft, about 10 to 20 minutes. Leave aside to cool slightly.

3. Put all the ingredients in a blender and purée until smooth. Return to the pan and reheat gently on low heat and stir in lemon juice.

4. Prior to serving, add 1 tablespoon of yoghurt and a garnish of chives to each soup bowl. Serve hot.

Turnip and Potato Soup

A simple, smooth and creamy soup with a pleasantly mild flavour.

Serves 4
125g (4oz) turnips, peeled and sliced
125g (4oz) potatoes, sliced but not peeled
1 large shallot, sliced
240ml (8fl.oz) vegetable stock
60g (2oz) butter
120ml (4fl.oz) milk, lowfat if preferred
a pinch of nutmeg

1. Heat half of the butter in a large saucepan. Add the shallot and sauté until soft, 5 minutes, stirring constantly.

2. Peel the turnips and slice thinly. Wash but do not peel the potatoes and slice them thinly also. Add the turnips and potatoes to the shallots and sauté the lot, stirring constantly, for 4 minutes.

3. Add the vegetable stock, bring to the boil and simmer covered until the potatoes are very tender, 15 to 20 minutes. Remove from the heat to cool slightly.

4. Place all the cooked ingredients in a blender and purée until smooth.

5. Return to the pan adding the milk with the rest of the butter, stirring well until hot, but not boiling. Stir in the nutmeg and serve piping hot.

Summerhouse Salads

Beetroot Salad with Chicory and Celery

This is a superbly colourful winter salad with a delightful pink tinge.

Serves 4-6
2 medium beetroots
4 large chicory heads
4 stalks of celery
2 tablespoons fresh coriander, finely chopped
2 tablespoons fresh parsley, finely chopped
for the vinaigrette dressing:
90ml (3fl.oz) olive oil
30ml (1fl.oz) white wine vinegar
2 teaspoons Dijon mustard
1 garlic clove, crushed or finely chopped

1. Trim away the tops, then cook the beetroots whole in boiling water until tender, up to 1 hour. Let them cool a little, then peel and cut into long thin strips.

2. Trim the stalk ends of the celery, pulling away any strings at the same time, then slice them thinly.

3. Trim off the bases of the chicory, wash well and remove any old or wilted leaves, then cut the heads into long thin strips.

4. Combine all the above vegetables into a mixing bowl, then prepare the vinaigrette dressing by mixing the oil, vinegar, mustard and garlic in a small bowl or cup and whisk thoroughly together. Pour the dressing over the vegetables and mix together well.

5. Transfer the mix to a salad bowl and sprinkle the coriander and parsley over the lot. Either serve immediately if cool enough, or refrigerate quickly before serving.

Cabbage and Caraway Salad

The subtle caraway flavour which permeates this salad, sets this one apart.

Serves 4
500g (1lb) white cabbage (1 small head), shredded
½ small onion, chopped finely
for the vinaigrette dressing:
2 tablespoons lemon juice (about 1 lemon)
90ml (3fl.oz) olive oil
30ml (1fl.oz) white wine vinegar
1 garlic clove, finely chopped
1 tablespoon caraway seeds

1. Mix the shredded cabbage and finely chopped onion together in a salad bowl.

2. Whisk the dressing ingredients thoroughly together. Pour the dressing over the vegetables and mix together well. Serve immediately.

Cucumber and Carrot Salad

A slightly spicy yet refreshing salad with an oriental feel.

Serves 4
1 medium long cucumber, finely sliced
3 small carrots, finely sliced
1 tablespoon sesame seeds

for the dressing:
1 teaspoon fresh ginger root, grated
2 tablespoons soy sauce
1 tablespoon white wine vinegar

1. Peel and wash the cucumber. Scrub and wash the carrots. Slice them both finely.

2. Mix together the ginger, soy sauce and vinegar, whisking thoroughly. Put the sesame seeds in a dry frying pan or under the grill and toast for a few minutes until golden brown.

3. Place the sliced cucumber and carrots in a salad bowl. Pour the dressing over the vegetables and sprinkle the sesame seeds on top. Mix well and serve chilled.

Fennel Salad with Walnuts

Serves 4-6
3 small fennel bulbs, finely sliced
fennel leaves, finely chopped
1 small shallot, finely sliced
125g (4oz) walnuts, chopped
1/4 teaspoon caraway seeds
1 tablespoon fresh thyme, finely chopped
boiling water
for the vinaigrette dressing:
90ml (3fl.oz) walnut oil
30ml (1fl.oz) white wine vinegar

1. Wash and remove any discoloured or wilted outer leaves of the fennel bulbs. Trim off the feathery leaves and chop them finely, keep aside. Finely slice the fennel bulbs.

2. Bring some water to the boil, drop in the finely sliced bulbs and boil until slightly soft, only 3 to 4 minutes. Immediately wash under cold water and let cool. Dry well on paper towels or a cloth.

3. Put the cooled fennel in a salad bowl. Add the shallot, walnuts, caraway seeds and thyme; mix well.

4. Whisk together the vinaigrette dressing ingredients. Pour this over the salad mixture and scatter the chopped fennel leaves as a garnish.

5. Just prior to serving, squeeze a little lemon juice over the lot. Serve chilled.

Lettuce Salad with Sugarsnap Peas and Chilli

The red chilli pepper gives this salad a pleasant 'bite', but can be excluded if you prefer it less fiery.

Serves 4
½ crispy lettuce, endive or similar
125g (4oz) sugarsnap peas
½ long English cucumber, sliced
1 shallot, finely sliced
for the dressing:
3 tablespoons olive oil
1 tablespoon cider vinegar
1 small fresh red chilli pepper, finely chopped (optional)
1 tablespoon fresh parsley, finely chopped
1 clove garlic, finely chopped

1. Wash and drain the lettuce well, removing any wilted leaves. Tear the freshest leaves into bite size pieces and put into a salad bowl.

2. Wash the peas, trim the ends and steam or drop them into boiling water until just tender, only 3 to 4 minutes. Drain and rinse under cold water, drain again.

3. Combine the cucumber, shallot and peas with the lettuce.

4. Combine all the dressing ingredients in a cup and whisk together vigorously. Immediately prior to serving, pour the dressing over the salad and toss well.

Lettuce Salad with Grapes and Cashews

This delicious salad could be a meal in itself - make plenty of it to go around!

Serves 4
150g (5oz) seedless grapes, black and green
125g (4oz) raw, unsalted cashews, halved
$^1/_2$ head crispy lettuce, such as endive
30g (1oz) butter
250g (8oz) cottage cheese, lowfat if preferred
for the dressing:
4 tablespoons peanut or groundnut oil
2 tablespoons lemon juice

1. Melt the butter in a small frying pan on medium heat. Add the cashews and cook until golden brown, shaking all the while, about 3 minutes. Drain on paper towels and set aside to cool.

2. Wash the lettuce leaves, tearing them into bite size pieces and shake dry. Place the leaves into a salad bowl and top with the cottage cheese and cashews.

3. Wash the grapes well, removing them from the stalks, then shake dry. Add these to the salad bowl.

4. Whisk together the oil and lemon juice in a small bowl. Pour this dressing over the salad ingredients, then toss everything together so the cottage cheese is mixed in well. Serve immediately.

New Season Potato Salad

The secret here is to use new potatoes, with their jackets intact.

Serves 4
500g (1lb) new potatoes
boiling water
for the dressing:
4 tablespoons mayonnaise, lowfat if preferred
1 teaspoon white wine vinegar
1 teaspoon Dijon mustard
1 tablespoon pickled gherkin (1 small gherkin), finely chopped
1 tablespoon natural yoghurt, lowfat if preferred
black pepper to taste, freshly ground

1. Wash and scrub the new potatoes. Place them whole in a saucepan of cold water then bring to the boil. Boil uncovered until just tender (not too soft), 10 to 15 minutes. Drain and leave to cool. Cut into bite-size pieces when cool enough. Put into a salad bowl.

2. In a small mixing bowl, combine all the dressing ingredients, mixing thoroughly.

3. Pour the dressing over the potatoes and toss until they are well coated. Serve immediately or later when chilled.

Radish Salad

Use small, fresh and crisp radishes for this slightly peppery salad.

Serves 4
1 bunch of small radishes, thinly sliced
2 tablespoons olive oil
black pepper to taste, freshly ground

1. Wash and scrub the radishes in cold water. Dry thoroughly with paper towels or a cloth. Slice them thinly.

2. Put them in a salad bowl and sprinkle with the olive oil and pepper. Chill briefly and serve immediately.

Vegetable Side-Plates

Cheesy Asparagus

Resplendent with cheese, this dish goes well with a refreshing crispy salad. As a spicy alternative, serve it with *Spicy Tomato Sauce (see page 74).*

Serves 4-6
750g (1½ lb) asparagus spears (20-25 spears)
30g (1oz) butter
500g (1lb) gruyère cheese, grated
2 tablespoons lemon juice
black pepper to taste, freshly ground
1 tablespoon chervil leaves, fresh
2-3 sprigs tarragon, fresh
a little olive oil or butter

1. Pre-heat the oven to 180°C, 350°F, gas mark 4. Lightly grease a casserole or oven dish with a little olive oil or butter.

2. Wash the asparagus spears, cutting off any woody ends and peeling the stalks if they appear to be a bit stringy. Simmer or steam the spears whole, until a little tender, about 4 to 5 minutes.

3. Drain the spears and arrange in the oven dish.

4. Break the butter into pieces and place evenly distributed across the spears. Pour the lemon juice over the asparagus and lay the chervil and tarragon around and on top of the spears.

5. Spread the grated cheese over the asparagus and bake for 10 minutes, making sure the asparagus is quite tender. Season with the black pepper before serving.

Asparagus Grilled

Grilled asparagus is most delicious when young, thin spears are used. But if only older, thicker spears are available, then peeling the tough outer skin of the stalks is necessary.

Serves 4
1kg (2lb) thin-medium asparagus spears (36-40 spears)
120ml (4fl.oz) olive oil
black pepper to taste, freshly ground
a handful of fresh savory sprigs
a handful of fresh rosemary sprigs

1. Wash thin asparagus spears and peel thick spears. Brush the spears all over with some of the olive oil. Place on a grilling tray and grill on medium heat for 2 or 3 minutes, turn to the other side and grill another few minutes until tender.

2. Heat the remaining olive oil in a frying pan, adding the fresh savory and rosemary. Allow the herb flavourings to diffuse into the oil on low heat, about 10 minutes or so.

3. Sprinkle the herb flavoured oil, with the herb sprigs, over the asparagus before serving.

Aubergines with Pesto

Mop up the olive oil with crunchy country bread and serve next to a main pasta or rice dish.

Serves 4
625g (1¼ lb) aubergines (2 medium-large), thinly sliced
salt
Italian Garden Pesto (see page 71)
for the vinaigrette dressing:
90ml (3fl.oz) olive oil
30ml (1fl.oz) white wine vinegar
2 teaspoons wholegrain mustard

1. Sprinkle salt over the aubergine slices so they are well covered. Leave for 20 to 30 minutes to draw out any bitterness.

2. Meanwhile, make the vinaigrette dressing by combining the oil, vinegar and mustard in a small bowl, whisking vigorously until mixed.

3. When ready, rinse the aubergines, drain and dry well with a cloth. Place the slices in a bowl, pour over the dressing and let the slices soak from 30 minutes to 2 hours.

4. Drain the dressing from the slices and pre-heat the grill. Place the slices on a grill tray and grill on a moderate heat until tender and pale brown, about 10 minutes. Turn over and grill the other side for the same time.

5. Spread one side of each slice with the pesto sauce and grill for another minute. Serve immediately while still hot.

Aubergine Fritters

These crispy fritters are ideal snacks for any time of the day, with or without a main meal.

Serves 4
625g (1¼ lb) aubergines (2 medium-large), thinly sliced
150g (5oz) wholemeal flour
240ml (8fl.oz) mild ale
peanut or groundnut oil, enough for frying
2 teaspoons dried thyme
coarse sea salt to taste (optional)

1. Peel the aubergines and cut into thin slices. Sprinkle each slice liberally with the dried thyme and pile on top of each other until they are ready for frying.

2. Sift the flour and whisk with the ale, creating a thin batter.

3. In a frying pan, pour the oil to about 5mm (¼in) depth and heat until the oil bubbles vigorously when a drop of water is placed in the pan.

4. Drop each aubergine slice into the batter so a thin layer surrounds the slice. Drop the battered slice into the hot oil. Let it cook until golden brown on one side then turn to cook the other side until golden brown also.

5. Drain the slices well on paper towels. If salt is desired, then sprinkle a little on each slice immediately prior to serving to ensure the aubergine slices retain their crispiness.

Green Beans with Almonds

Serves 4
500g (1lb) thin green beans
60g (2oz) slivered almonds
4 tablespoons double cream
4 tablespoons almond oil
lemon juice
black pepper to taste, freshly ground

1. Trim both ends of the beans and string them if necessary. Cut each in half, wash and drain them. Steam them until just tender, about 5 minutes and drain under cold water.

2. Lightly toast the almonds by either placing them on a tray under the grill or putting them in a dry frying pan and shaking until golden brown.

3. Mix the cream and almond oil in a bowl, seasoning with the black pepper.

4. Add the beans into the cream mix, mixing well.

5. Sprinkle the toasted almonds over the beans, with a little lemon juice. Serve cool but not refrigerated.

Green Beans with Onion

Serves 4
500g (1lb) thin green beans
30g (1oz) butter
1 small onion, finely chopped
1 clove garlic, finely chopped
½ teaspoon dried thyme
1 tablespoon fresh parsley, chopped
black pepper to taste, freshly ground

1. Trim both ends of the beans, removing any strings. Steam until just tender, about 5 minutes or so.

2. Meanwhile, melt the butter in a frying pan on medium heat. Add the onion and cook until tender and translucent, 3 to 5 minutes. Add the garlic and cook for 2 more minutes, stirring constantly.

3. Drain the beans, add to the frying pan and stir in the thyme and black pepper. Cook on medium heat for another 3 minutes, stirring all ingredients well. Sprinkle with the parsley and serve immediately when hot.

Buttered Bothy Beans

Fresh broad beans are most delicious when young, but older ones can be just as tasty when you peel away the tough outer skin of each individual bean. Make sure you prepare this dish at the last minute in order to retain as much freshness as possible.

Serves 4
2kg (4lb) broad beans
60g (2oz) butter
240ml (8fl.oz) vegetable stock
2 tablespoons fresh parsley, chopped
1 sprig of fresh thyme
black pepper to taste, freshly ground

1. Shell the beans and if necessary, remove the tough outer skin with a small sharp knife.

2. In a small saucepan, bring the vegetable stock to the boil. Add the beans, thyme and a quarter of the butter, boil uncovered for about 5 minutes.

3. Remove the thyme and add the remaining butter and parsley, cooking until the liquid has reduced and the sauce becomes slightly thickened and creamy. Season with the black pepper and serve hot.

Brussels Sprouts with Garlic

Fresh, young, new season Brussels sprouts have a delicate flavour when cooked quickly and simply. Pay close attention to the cooking time of the sprouts - it's better to have them ever so slightly undercooked rather than at all overdone.

Serves 4
500g (1lb) small Brussels sprouts
boiling water
4 garlic cloves, finely chopped
3 tablespoons olive oil
30g (1oz) extra mature cheddar cheese, grated
black pepper to taste, freshly ground
lemon juice

1. Wash and remove any wilted leaves from the sprouts. Cut a small cross in the base of each sprout with a sharp knife. Steam or boil them until almost tender, about 5 minutes. Drain.

2. Meanwhile, heat the oil in a large frying pan and add the garlic. Sauté the garlic for 2 minutes, stirring constantly.

3. Add the drained sprouts to the garlic in the pan and season with the black pepper. Cook for a few minutes on low heat stirring until the sprouts are well coated with the oil and garlic.

4. prinkle with lemon juice while still in the pan and cook for another minute. Turn off the heat and add the grated cheese to the sprouts in the pan. Mix gently so the cheese is slightly melted. Serve immediately.

Brussels Sprouts and Chestnuts

Try to use *fresh* chestnuts for this classic combination.

Serves 4

500g (1lb) small Brussels sprouts
250g (8oz) fresh chestnuts
30g (1oz) butter
black pepper to taste, freshly ground
lemon juice

1. Wash and remove any wilted leaves from the sprouts. Cut a small cross in the base of each sprout with a sharp knife. Steam or boil them until only just tender, 8 to 10 minutes. Drain.

2. Meanwhile, skin the chestnuts by simmering for 10 minutes or placing them in a hot oven at 290°C, 550°F, gas mark 9 for 15 minutes. Once cooked, the skin should be easily peeled with the help of a sharp knife.

3. Melt the butter in a small frying pan and gently fry the peeled chestnuts on low heat. While cooking, break the chestnuts into large pieces. Cook until golden brown, 10 minutes or so.

4. Add the cooked sprouts to the chestnuts in the pan and add some extra butter if all has been absorbed. Sprinkle with a little lemon juice and season with pepper just prior to serving. Serve hot.

Annabel's Red Cabbage

A spicy yet sweet combination, this red cabbage dish served hot, goes especially well with potatoes.

Serves 4-6
500g (1lb) red cabbage (1 small head), shredded
1 medium onion, sliced
1 small cooking apple
1 small dessert apple
30g (1oz) butter
2-3 teaspoons unrefined sugar
2-3 teaspoons red wine vinegar
4 whole cloves
black pepper to taste, freshly ground
a little water

1. Melt the butter in a small frying pan, add the onion and sauté until soft, 5 to 6 minutes, stirring constantly.

2. Peel and slice the apples. Transfer the onion to a large saucepan and add the shredded cabbage, sugar, vinegar, cloves, pepper and apples. Add enough water to cover the bottom of the pan to avoid it burning. Cover the pan tightly and cook on low heat for up to 2 hours, until very soft.

3. During the cooking, stir all the ingredients and taste for more sugar or vinegar as necessary. Serve hot.

Cardoons with Garlic Butter

Due to their rather delicate taste, cardoons are best complemented by strongly flavoured sauces, such as this garlic butter one.

Serves 4
8 stems cardoon, thickly sliced
8 cloves garlic, finely chopped
90g (3oz) butter
2 tablespoons olive oil
black pepper to taste, freshly ground
boiling water
2 tablespoons lemon juice
60g (2oz) extra mature cheddar cheese, grated (optional)

1. Trim the cardoon stem ends, pulling off any strings at the same time. Cut into large pieces, about 5cm (2in) long.

2. Bring to the boil enough water to cover the stems and add the lemon juice. Place the stems in the boiling water and simmer until tender, 15 to 20 minutes. Drain well.

3. Meanwhile, heat the oil and butter in a frying pan on low heat. Add the garlic, season generously with black pepper and sauté gently until the liquid becomes slightly creamy.

4. Pour the garlic sauce over the cooked cardoons and serve hot.

optional:
Just prior to serving, sprinkle the grated cheese over the sauce on the cardoons and grill under medium heat until golden brown. Serve immediately.

Baked Chicory with Herby Cheese Sauce

An elegantly aromatic method of treating chicory.

Serves 4
8 chicory heads (2 per person)
a pinch of nutmeg
black pepper to taste, freshly ground
4 tablespoons olive oil
2 tablespoons lemon juice
300ml (10fl.oz) vegetable stock
16 sprigs fresh rosemary
16 sprigs fresh thyme
for the cheese sauce:
300ml (10fl.oz) milk, lowfat if preferred
2 tablespoons wholemeal flour
45g (1 1/2 oz) butter
black pepper to taste, freshly ground
a pinch of cayenne pepper
60g (2oz) extra mature cheddar cheese, grated

1. Pour the olive oil into a casserole or oven dish so the base is covered. Pre-heat the oven to 200°C, 400°F, gas mark 6.

2. Trim off the base of each chicory head and remove any discoloured or wilted outer leaves. Put the chicory heads in the casserole dish and roll them around in the oil to ensure they are well covered.

3. Whisk the lemon juice and nutmeg into the vegetable stock then pour this liquid over the chicory heads. Arrange the herb sprigs around the chicory and season generously with black pepper.

4. Cover the dish with aluminium foil and bake until the chicory is tender, 40 minutes to an hour. Meanwhile, prepare the cheese sauce.

For the cheese sauce:

5. Sift the flour. Place all the ingredients (except the cheese and cayenne pepper) together and blend until smooth, about 15 seconds. Pour this sauce into a medium saucepan and heat gently, stirring constantly.

6. Bring to the boil, but immediately reduce the heat and simmer, adding the cheese and stirring constantly. Simmer for another five minutes to allow the flour to cook. Set aside until needed.

7. When the chicory is cooked, pour the cooking juices into the cheese sauce. Heat up the sauce, add the cayenne pepper, then mix well. Pour this sauce over the chicory and serve immediately while hot.

Grilled Courgettes with Parmesan

Grilled in this way, the courgettes will remain slightly crunchy, retaining their mild, nutty flavour. Serve with *Spicy Tomato Sauce (see page 74)* and most importantly, serve immediately after cooking, while hot.

Serves 4
8 medium courgettes (2 per person), halved
2 cloves garlic, finely chopped
125g (4oz) parmesan cheese, grated
$^1/_2$ teaspoon black pepper, freshly ground
olive oil

1. Wash the courgettes and cut each in half lengthways. Brush each side with olive oil and grill on medium heat for 5 minutes on each side.

2. Mix together the garlic, parmesan and black pepper. Sprinkle this mix evenly over the cut half of each slice. Grill on medium heat until golden brown, 6 to 8 minutes.

3. Meanwhile, heat the *Spicy Tomato Sauce* and pour over the courgettes. Serve immediately.

Baked Garlic with Herb Cheese

Consuming whole garlic bulbs may seem at first a daunting experience, but the sweet, nutty flavour combined with the aromatic herbed cheese this recipe offers is a surprising delight. Incidentally, any leftover herbed cheese is superb on bread or dried biscuits. (A hint: use a muffin pan to hold each bulb upright during cooking.)

Serves 4
4 whole bulb heads of garlic (1 per person)
4 tablespoons olive oil
4 tablespoons water
4 dried bay leaves
4 sprigs fresh rosemary
4 sprigs fresh thyme
for the herb cheese:
300g (10oz) cottage cheese, lowfat if preferred
30g (1oz) mixed fresh herbs: tarragon, chives, chervil, basil, finely chopped

1. Trim the roots off the base of each garlic bulb and cut off the skin on the tips of the cloves. Pre-heat the oven to 180°C, 350°F, gas mark 4.

2. Place individual bulbs into each muffin hollow in an upright position. Pour 1 tablespoon of water around each bulb. Pour 1 tablespoon of olive oil over each bulb and place one sprig of each herb around each bulb.

3. Cover with aluminium foil and bake for 30 minutes. Uncover and bake further for another 10 to 15 minutes, until the garlic is tender when pressed.

4. Meanwhile, prepare the herb cheese. Finely chop the fresh, mixed herbs. Combine the cottage cheese and chopped herbs in a small bowl, mixing well.

5. Serve the garlic bulbs with the cooking juices poured over them on individual plates. Use a fork to remove each clove from its shell, or squeeze out between your fingers. Serve the herbed cheese in small bowls on the side for dipping the cloves into.

Globe Artichokes and Mushrooms

Serve as an intriguing appetiser or an accompaniment to a rice and vegetable dish. (A hint: make sure all the prickly tips of the leaves are removed before cooking).

Serves 4
4 large globe artichokes
125g (4oz) mushrooms, finely chopped
30g (1oz) butter
black pepper to taste, freshly ground
1 tablespoon garlic chives, finely chopped
boiling water
1 egg yolk
120ml (4fl.oz) single cream
2 tablespoons lemon juice (about 1 lemon)

1. Pull off the stems and cut off the spiny leaf tips of the globe artichokes. Bring a large saucepan of water to the boil and place the artichokes in so the water just covers. Simmer uncovered for 30 minutes or so until tender.

2. Whisk the egg yolk with a fork or blender, add the cream, mixing well. Whisk in the lemon juice.

3. Heat the butter on a moderate heat in a frying pan, add the mushrooms. Stir constantly and cook for a few minutes. Add the pepper and garlic chives, cooking for 2 more minutes.

4. Add the egg/cream mix to the mushrooms, stirring over low heat, do not boil.

5. Once the artichokes are tender, cut each in half lengthways and remove the prickly 'choke' from the centre, being careful to retain the tender heart beneath.

6. Pour somc of the sauce over the opened halves, and the rest of the sauce on the side. Serve immediately.

Globe Artichokes with Asparagus and Green Olive Sauce

Serves 4
4 large globe artichokes
8 medium asparagus spears
170g (6oz) pitted green olives, finely chopped
30g (1oz) butter
2 tablespoons parmesan cheese, grated
a pinch of ground nutmeg
black pepper to taste, freshly ground
450ml (15fl.oz) boiling water

1. Pull off the stems and cut off the spiny leaf tips of the globe artichokes. Bring a large saucepan of water to the boil and place the artichokes in so the water just covers. Simmer uncovered for 30 minutes or so until tender.

2. Peel the asparagus stalks and cut into thick slices. Cut off the tips, putting to one side for later.

3. Melt the butter in a saucepan on low heat, add the sliced asparagus stalks and cook covered for about 5 minutes until just tender. Add the chopped green olives and nutmeg. Lightly mix altogether in the pan, cover and cook on low until heated through. Remove from the heat, keeping warm.

4. Meanwhile, boil the water in a small saucepan. Place the asparagus tips in the boiling water and cook uncovered until tender, 5 to 6 minutes. Once cooked, drain and pour cold water over them. Cut the tips in half lengthwise and keep for later.

5. Once the artichokes are tender, cut each in half lengthways and remove the prickly 'choke' from the centre, being careful to retain the tender heart beneath. Also remove some of the tiny central leaves to create a small hollow. Place the artichoke halves in a baking dish, with the cut sides facing up.

6. Fill the artichoke halves with the asparagus-olive mixture, using a spoon to press down the mixture firmly.

7. Mix together the ground black pepper and parmesan cheese. Sprinkle quite thickly over the top of each half. Grill on a moderate heat until golden, 5 to 10 minutes.

8. Meanwhile, reheat the asparagus tips and place on top of each half as decoration. Serve immediately.

Jerusalem Artichokes tossed in Breadcrumbs

Serve with a rice or pasta main meal, and be careful not to overcook the Jerusalem artichokes.

Serves 4
250g (8oz) Jerusalem artichokes
60g (2oz) butter
60g (2oz) wholemeal breadcrumbs
black pepper to taste, freshly ground
boiling water
1 tablespoon fresh parsley, finely chopped
lemon juice

1. Peel and wash the Jerusalem artichokes, cut into bite-size pieces. Place them in a pan of cold water just covering, bring to the boil and cook until only just tender, 5 to 8 minutes. Drain and keep aside.

2. Melt the butter in a medium frying pan. Add the breadcrumbs and black pepper, and cook on medium heat for 6 to 8 minutes, stirring constantly. Add the cooked and sliced artichokes to the breadcrumbs, toss them until coated well and heated through.

3. Sprinkle with chopped parsley and a little lemon juice. Serve immediately while hot.

Kale with Onion and Garlic Purée

A lovely winter vegetable accompaniment with lots of garlic to combat those winter colds.

Serves 4-6
500g (1lb) kale
boiling water
Onion and Garlic Purée (see page 72)
fresh parsley, finely chopped

1. While preparing the purée, wash and rinse the kale well. Remove any discoloured or wilted leaves. Bring enough water (to just cover the kale) to the boil. Place the kale in the boiling water and simmer until cooked through, 5 to 10 minutes. Drain and dry with paper towels or a cloth.

2. Reheat the purée until hot. Serve the kale on individual plates and pour the onion and garlic purée over the leaves. Sprinkle with the chopped parsley and serve hot.

Kohlrabi, Cream and Spice

Kohlrabi has a crunchy texture with a slight cabbage flavour which combines well with cream and plenty of spices.

Serves 4-6
750g (1½ lb) kohlrabi, sliced
30g (1oz) butter
240ml (8fl.oz) vegetable stock
4 teaspoons wholemeal flour
240ml (8fl.oz) double cream
1 teaspoon fresh coriander, finely chopped
2 tablespoons fresh parsley, finely chopped
3 sprigs fresh rosemary
black pepper to taste, freshly ground
½ teaspoon mustard powder
a pinch of chilli powder

1. Peel the kohlrabi and slice into thick wedges. Wash and drain.

2. Melt the butter in a large saucepan over medium heat and add the sliced kohlrabi. Stir constantly and cook for about 2 minutes before adding the vegetable stock.

3. Season the stock and kohlrabi generously with black pepper, and add the rosemary sprigs, mustard and chilli powders. Cover and simmer over low heat until the kohlrabi is just tender, about 10 minutes.

4. Stir the flour into the cream in a separate bowl.

5. Remove the rosemary sprigs from the saucepan, then add the flour-cream mixture to the kohlrabi and combine well.

6. Stir in the parsley and coriander and simmer over low heat until the cream has thickened slightly, another 5 to 10 minutes. Stir constantly and make sure the sauce is heated right through. Serve immediately while piping hot.

Leaf Beet (Swiss Chard) and Onions

As with most green leafy recipes, spinach may be used in place of the leaf beet.

Serves 4
875g (1¾ lb) leaf beet (Swiss chard), stalks and leaves
2 medium white onions, sliced
1 clove garlic, finely chopped
3-4 tablespoons olive oil
boiling water
1 teaspoon sesame seeds, toasted
1 tablespoon fresh coriander, finely chopped
black pepper to taste, freshly ground
500g (1lb) ricotta cheese

1. Heat 2 tablespoons olive oil in a large frying pan on low heat, add onions and sauté gently on low heat until very soft, 10 to 15 minutes.

2. Meanwhile, remove the leaves from the stalks with a sharp knife, wash and leave them to drain.

3. Bring a small saucepan of water to the boil. Trim the stalk ends and remove any strings at the same time. Cut the stalks into thick wedges and drop into the boiling water, simmer until tender, 10 to 15 minutes. Set aside and let the cooking juices soak into the stalks for 10 minutes before draining.

4. Meanwhile, add the drained leaves to the sautéed onions on low heat until the bulk is reduced and the leaves are well coated in olive oil and onion.

5. In a dry frying pan or in a tray under the grill, lightly toast the sesame seeds until golden brown.

6. Drain the stalks and add these to the onion-leaf mixture, stir in well. Add the garlic and sesame seeds, cooking for another 5 minutes, stirring constantly. Season with pepper to taste.
7. Sprinkle with the chopped coriander leaves and serve with a few tablespoons of ricotta cheese on the side.

Baked Leeks with Aromatics

This fragrant recipe, generous in herbs and spices, goes particularly well with tomato and rice dishes.

Serves 4
8 medium-thick leeks (2 per person)
2 cloves garlic, finely chopped
1 teaspoon caraway seeds
1 teaspoon coriander powder
1 teaspoon black pepper, freshly ground
1 bay leaf
2 sprigs fresh winter savory
4-5 tablespoons olive oil
450ml (15fl.oz) vegetable stock
juice of 1 lemon

1. Trim the root ends of the leeks and discard the green parts, wash and drain.

2. In a dry frying pan or on a tray under the grill, toast the caraway seeds for a few minutes, then grind them to a powder.

3. Bring the vegetable stock to the boil in a small saucepan, then add the toasted caraway seeds, coriander powder, bay leaf, garlic and winter savory. Cover the pan and remove from the heat, leave for 10 minutes or so for the herbs to infuse.

4. Place the leeks in a shallow saucepan and pour the infused stock over them. Add the lemon juice and olive oil. Cover and cook over low heat until the leeks are nicely tender, 20 to 30 minutes. Remove the leeks and keep in a warm serving dish.

5. Strain the cooking juices and simmer, uncovered for a few minutes until the liquid has reduced slightly. Pour over the leeks and serve immediately while hot.

Leek and Herby Cheese Ramekin Pies

Serve with spicy chutney or *Spicy Tomato Sauce (see page 74).*

Serves 4
500g (1lb) leeks, finely sliced
1 clove garlic, finely chopped
4 eggs, lightly beaten
60g (2oz) breadcrumbs
125g (4oz) extra mature cheddar cheese, grated
1 tablespoon olive oil
½ tablespoon fresh parsley, finely chopped
½ tablespoon fresh savory, finely chopped
black pepper to taste, freshly ground

1. Pre-heat the oven to 200°C, 400°F, gas mark 6. Heat the oil in a small saucepan on low heat, add the sliced leeks and chopped garlic and cook until soft, 10 minutes. Stir constantly.

2. In a small mixing bowl, mix together the eggs, grated cheese, breadcrumbs, parsley and savory. Add the cooked leeks and garlic, with their cooking juices. Season with black pepper.

3. Line four ramekin dishes with aluminium foil or greaseproof paper. Pour the batter evenly into the dishes. Bake for 15 to 20 minutes until firm, but not too dry. When cooked, turn out the ramekins from the dishes and serve immediately while hot.

Herb-baked Marrow Chunks

An excellent way of dealing with marrow, using a marvellous blend of herbs and spices.

Serves 4
1 large marrow
60g (2oz) butter
1/2 teaspoon dried oregano
1/2 teaspoon dried tarragon
1/2 teaspoon fennel seeds
1/2 teaspoon cumin seeds
1/2 teaspoon coriander seeds
black pepper to taste, freshly ground

1. Lightly grease a shallow casserole or oven dish with some of the butter. Pre-heat the oven to 170°C, 425°F, gas mark 3.

2. Peel and wash the marrow, remove the seeds and surrounding pith. Cut the marrow flesh into bite size pieces and place them into the bottom of the oven dish in a single layer.

3. Crush the fennel, cumin and coriander seeds together and sprinkle over the marrow pieces evenly, along with the herbs and pepper. Break up the butter into small pieces and spread evenly over the lot.

4. Cover with aluminium foil and bake for 30 to 35 minutes. Remove the foil, turn the marrow pieces over and bake another 10 minutes. Serve immediately while hot.

Baked Stuffed Mushrooms

This is very quick and simple, especially for those of us who normally wouldn't bother stuffing a mushroom!

Serves 4
8 large mushrooms (2 per person)
2 cloves garlic, finely chopped
2 tablespoons olive oil
125g (4oz) breadcrumbs
1 egg
1 $^{1}/_{2}$ tablespoons fresh coriander, finely chopped
60g (2oz) extra mature cheddar cheese, grated
black pepper to taste, freshly ground

1. Pre-heat the oven to 180°C, 350°F, gas mark 4. Remove the mushroom stems and slice finely, keeping them aside. Scoop out a little of the insides of the mushrooms and keep these bits aside. Brush the mushroom top with some olive oil and place on a baking tray.

2. In a mixing bowl, combine the garlic, breadcrumbs, coriander, black pepper, mushroom stems and mushroom centres. Lightly beat the egg with a fork and add to this mixture.

3. Spoon the egg/spice filling evenly into the scooped-out mushroom tops, putting as much filling as you possibly can into each. Press down firmly and sprinkle the grated cheese over this. Bake for 10 to 15 minutes. Serve immediately while hot.

Parsnip Fritters

A very tasty and creative parsnip dish.

Serves 4
500g (1lb) parsnips, chopped
1 clove garlic, finely chopped
1 small onion, finely chopped
3 tablespoons olive oil
1 egg
black pepper to taste, freshly ground
a pinch of ground nutmeg

1. Wash and scrub the parsnips, then chop into chunks. Place in a saucepan in cold water and bring to the boil. Simmer until tender, 15 to 20 minutes.

2. Heat 1 tablespoon of oil in a small frying pan, add the onion and sauté until translucent, 5 minutes, then add the garlic and cook another 2 minutes.

3. Purée the parsnips in a blender with some of the cooking water and leave aside to cool. Make sure this purée is not too watery.

4. Lightly beat the egg with the ground nutmeg and black pepper. In a mixing bowl, combine this with the sautéed onions and garlic. Add the parsnip purée and stir together.

5. Heat the rest of the oil in a frying pan on medium-hot heat. Drop large spoonsful of the parsnip mixture into the hot oil, pressing down with a spatula. Cook on both sides until golden brown, about 5 minutes each side.

6. Drain well on paper towels and serve hot.

Mange-tout Peas with Red Pepper

Naturally sweet, crispy and colourful.

Serves 4
500g (1lb) mange-tout peas
1 red bell pepper, sliced
2 medium oranges, juice and rind
75g (2 1/2 oz) butter
black pepper to taste, freshly ground

1. Trim away the internal membranes and remove the seeds from the red pepper. Skin the pepper by cutting into quarters and placing skin-side up under the grill. Once black and blistered, remove from the grill and easily peel away the skin. Rinse under cold water, drain, then slice into long thin strips.

2. Wash and drain the peas. Trim the ends and pull away any strings at the same time. Steam or place the peas in boiling water until just tender, only 3 to 4 minutes. Drain them under cold running water to refresh.

3. Wash and dry the oranges, peel the rind from one orange. Squeeze both oranges and put the juice into a medium saucepan, add the orange rind. Boil this liquid for a few minutes until slightly reduced in volume, then remove the rind and stir in the butter, whisking quickly until fluffy.

4. Add the peas and pepper to the orange sauce, season with black pepper and heat until warmed through. Serve on warmed plates.

Chunky Mashed Potatoes with Black Olives

When eating home-made mashed potatoes, it's much more interesting to encounter some chunky pieces, so don't mash these too finely.

Serves 4
500g (1lb) potatoes, peeled and sliced
30g (1oz) butter
125g (4oz) black olives, pitted
boiling water

1. Peel the potatoes, wash and slice them. Place them in a saucepan of cold water and bring to the boil. Boil them uncovered until tender, 10 to 15 minutes.

2. Coarsely mash the potatoes in the pan with a fork over low heat, and mix in the butter until melted.

3. Slice the olives thinly and stir into the potatoes. Serve immediately while hot.

Scorzonera in Cheese Sauce

This recipe is definitely best when served piping hot.

Serves 4
16 roots scorzonera
4 tablespoons breadcrumbs
30g (1oz) mature cheddar cheese, grated
boiling water
for the cheese sauce:
300ml (10fl.oz) milk, lowfat if preferred
2 tablespoons wholemeal flour
45g (1 1/2 oz) butter
black pepper to taste, freshly ground
a pinch of cayenne pepper
60g (2oz) extra mature cheddar cheese, grated

1. Wash off any clinging soil and cut each root into 2.5cm (1in) length pieces.

2. Bring enough water (to cover the scorzonera) to the boil in a medium saucepan. Place the unpeeled pieces into the water and simmer uncovered until only just tender, 15 to 20 minutes. Drain in cold water, then peel off the skin which should come away easily.

Meanwhile, prepare the cheese sauce:

3. Sift the flour. Place all the ingredients (except the cheese and cayenne pepper) together and blend until smooth. Pour the blended liquid into a medium saucepan and gently heat, stirring constantly.

4. Bring to the boil, then immediately reduce the heat and simmer, adding the cheese and stirring constantly. Simmer for another 5 minutes to allow the flour to cook. Add the cayenne pepper just prior to serving.

5. Place the cooked scorzonera (still hot) in a warmed serving dish. Pour the hot cheese sauce over the lot. Sprinkle the extra grated cheese and breadcrumbs evenly over the top and grill on high heat until golden brown, a few minutes. Serve immediately when piping hot.

Fried Salsify

Serves 4
1kg (2lb) salsify
250g (8oz) wholemeal flour
120ml (4fl.oz) olive oil
boiling water
1 teaspoon ground nutmeg
black pepper to taste, freshly ground

1. Wash and scrub the salsify thoroughly. Trim the ends and cut into 5cm (2in) pieces. Place them into boiling water and boil uncovered until just tender, 15 to 20 minutes.

2. Sift the flour. Combine the nutmeg and pepper with the flour in a mixing bowl. Toss the cooked salsify into the flour mixture until well coated.

3. Heat the oil in a deep pan until quite hot. Drop the salsify pieces into the oil and cook until golden, turning all the while. Drain well on paper towels and serve while hot.

Roast Shallots

Whole roasted shallots make neat and simple companions to a roast or baked meal.

Serves 4
500g (1lb) medium red shallots
2 tablespoons butter
black pepper to taste, freshly ground

1. Pre-heat the oven to 140°C, 275°F, gas mark 1. Trim the ends of the shallots and wash well. Place in a baking tray and bake until tender, 30 to 40 minutes.

2. Peel them when done and toss in melted butter, seasoning with black pepper.

Spinach and Pinenut Kernels

Especially for those who love the rich flavour of spinach. Serve together with crunchy country baked bread and a fresh crispy salad.

Serves 4

1kg (2lb) spinach leaves
60g (2oz) pinenut kernels
1 tablespoon olive oil
2 cloves garlic, finely chopped
1 tablespoon lemon juice
$^1/_2$ teaspoon ground nutmeg
1-2 tablespoons soy sauce

1. Heat the oil in a large frying pan, add the garlic and sauté on low heat for 3 minutes.

2. Wash the spinach thoroughly, changing the water at least once. Tear the spinach into large pieces and place in the frying pan gradually as the bulk reduces, until it all fits in.

3. Add the remaining ingredients, stir well, cover. Cook for 1 more minute then serve.

Grilled Spring Onions

Use the largest spring onions you can find and serve with some rustic home-made bread to soak up the olive oil.

Serves 4

4 large spring onions
a little olive oil
lemon or lime juice

1. Trim away the ends of the spring onions and wash well. Coat them with olive oil.

2. Place on a grilling tray and grill under medium heat until golden brown on both sides and tender, about 6 to 8 minutes. Serve immediately with a sprinkle of lemon or lime juice.

Stokehole Delight (Spicy Mashed Swedes)

A spiced-up version of the well-known traditional dish.

Serves 4
1kg (2lb) swedes, peeled
1 clove garlic, finely chopped
boiling water
60g (2oz) butter
3 tablespoons vegetable stock
a pinch of cayenne pepper
a pinch of ground nutmeg
black pepper to taste, freshly ground

1. Peel and wash the swedes. Cut into small chunks. Bring enough water to the boil to cover the swedes and cook until very tender, 10 minutes. Drain.

2. Place the swedes, garlic and vegetable stock into a blender and purée until smooth.

3. Put the purée into a saucepan and heat gently. Stir in the spices and butter, beating with a wooden spoon until heated through. Add more butter if the mix is a little dry. Serve immediately when hot.

Cherry Tomatoes and Basil

Ever so sweet and juicy, cherry tomatoes blend perfectly with the aromatic flavour of fresh basil leaves. Serve with fresh crispy, home-made bread to mop up the herbed oil.

Serves 4
500g (1lb) cherry tomatoes
20-24 fresh basil leaves, finely chopped
1/2 teaspoon fresh thyme leaves
2 tablespoons fresh parsley, finely chopped
1 clove garlic, finely chopped
3 tablespoons olive oil
black pepper to taste, freshly ground

1. Remove the tomato stems and wash well. Dry with paper towels or a cloth.

2. Mix together the garlic, basil and parsley.

3. Heat the oil in a large frying pan on high heat, then add the tomatoes. Immediately add the garlic-herb mixture, thyme and black pepper. Lift the pan and shake until the tomatoes are coated with the hot herb-oil mix. Heat through for only 1 to 2 minutes until the tomatoes are warmed through, yet still firm.

4. Serve immediately while hot.

Hearty Main Dishes

Broccoli and Pasta

A very tasty combination to form a lovely filling meal – the olives provide an inspirational touch.

Serves 6
2 medium onions, chopped finely
750g ($1^{1}/_{2}$lb) broccoli, chopped coarsely
250g (8oz) cherry tomatoes
8 cloves garlic, finely chopped
90g (3oz) pinenut kernels
125g (4oz) black olives, pitted
2-3 tablespoons olive oil
480ml (16fl.oz) water
2 tablespoons wholemeal flour
375g (12oz) pasta such as tagliatelle
parmesan cheese, grated
black pepper to taste, freshly ground

1. Heat the olive oil in a small frying pan. Add the onions and sauté until very soft, about 10 minutes, stirring constantly. Transfer to a large saucepan once done.

2. Roughly chop the broccoli heads then peel and chop the stems. Add the broccoli and water to the saucepan. On medium heat, simmer until the broccoli is just tender, about 5 minutes. Bring it to the boil and whisk in the flour until it is dissolved.

3. Turn down the heat to low and add the cherry tomatoes, olives and garlic. Keep this sauce warm on low heat so all the ingredients are heated through and the flour is cooked, stirring occasionally.

4. Meanwhile, boil the pasta and drain. Serve the pasta with the sauce spooned on top with some grated parmesan and black pepper sprinkled liberally over the lot. Serve hot.

Cauliflower and Ricotta Pie with Potato Crust

Serve with a refreshing lettuce or cabbage salad.

Serves 4

1 medium cauliflower, thinly sliced
1 onion, finely chopped
30g (1oz) butter
1 tablespoon wholemeal flour
4 eggs
½ teaspoon dried marjoram
½ teaspoon dried thyme
a pinch of cayenne pepper
black pepper to taste, freshly ground
250g (8oz) ricotta cheese
60g (2oz) parmesan cheese, grated

for the crust:

400g (13oz) potatoes (2 large potatoes), grated
60g (2oz) onion (½ onion), grated
1 egg white, lightly beaten
½ teaspoon salt
a little olive oil

For the crust:

1. Pre-heat the oven to 200°C, 400°F, gas mark 6 and oil a casserole or pie dish.

2. Wash and grate the potatoes (without peeling). Peel and grate the onion. Combine all the crust ingredients in a mixing bowl. Spread this mixture evenly into the oven dish, lining the base and edges.

3. Bake for 20 to 30 minutes until golden brown, then brush with a little olive oil and return to the oven. Bake for another 10 minutes, being careful not to burn the edges.

For the filling:

4. Turn the oven down to 190°C, 375°F, gas mark 5.

5. Steam or boil the thinly sliced cauliflower until almost tender, 5 to 6 minutes. Drain.

6. Melt the butter in a medium saucepan and fry the onion for 3 to 4 minutes. Add the cooked cauliflower, flour and herbs to the onion, mix well and cook for one minute.

7. Beat together the ricotta, parmesan, eggs, cayenne and black pepper. Add this mix to the cooked cauliflower mixture and combine well.

8. Spoon the cauliflower mixture into the cooked potato crust. Bake for 15 to 20 minutes, until the eggs have set. Serve immediately.

Spicy Cauliflower Casserole

This is a highly flavoured dish with lots of delicious herbs and spices.

Serves 4-6
1 medium-large cauliflower, thinly sliced
450ml (15fl.oz) Spicy Tomato Sauce (see page 74)
1 small onion, chopped
3 cloves garlic, finely chopped
1 tablespoon fresh ginger root, finely chopped
2 tablespoons fresh coriander, finely chopped
a pinch of ground cinnamon
black pepper to taste, freshly ground
3 tablespoons breadcrumbs
250g (8oz) extra mature cheddar cheese, grated
1 tablespoon olive oil

1. Slice the cauliflower thinly, including any stems. Steam or boil until just tender, 5-6 minutes. Drain and set aside.

2. Pre-heat the oven to 200°C, 400°F, gas mark 6. Lightly oil a casserole or oven dish.

3. Heat the olive oil in a medium frying pan and gently sauté the onion for 5 minutes. Add the garlic, ginger, cinnamon and black pepper, and stirring constantly, cook for another 3 minutes.

4. Put the cooked cauliflower in a mixing bowl and add the cooked onion mix, combining well. Mix in the *Spicy Tomato Sauce* and coriander, stirring well then spoon this mixture into the oven dish.

5. Combine the breadcrumbs and cheese in a small bowl and sprinkle evenly over the top of the mix in the oven dish. Bake uncovered until golden brown on top, 20-30 minutes. Serve immediately, while hot.

Celeriac and Potato Pancake Cribs

Serve these crispy pancakes with a cool, refreshing salad and some lightly cooked green vegetables.

Serves 4
2 large potatoes, grated
250g (8oz) celeriac (1 small celeriac root), grated
60g (2oz) butter
1 tablespoon peanut or groundnut oil
black pepper to taste, freshly ground
1 medium white onion, thinly sliced
a pinch of ground nutmeg
60g (2oz) extra mature cheddar cheese, grated

1. Peel and grate both the celeriac and potatoes. Combine in a mixing bowl.

2. Heat the oil and butter in a frying pan on medium heat. Divide the mixture into 4 to 6 portions and roll into balls with your hands. Place these balls into the hot oil and flatten them with a spatula once in the pan.

3. Cook on one side for about 10 minutes until golden brown, then turn over and cook another 10 minutes or so. Remove from the oil when cooked and drain well on paper towels.

4. Meanwhile, finely slice the onion and grate the cheese. Mix together the onion, cheese, black pepper and nutmeg. Sprinkle this mixture on top of the drained pancakes, then grill under medium heat until golden on top, about 5 minutes. Serve immediately.

Leaf Beet (Swiss Chard) and Cheese Omelette

Makes an ideal breakfast, lunch or dinner meal.

Makes 2 omelettes
250g (8oz) leaf beet (Swiss chard), leaves only
1 large onion, sliced
2-3 tablespoons olive oil
60g (2oz) extra mature cheddar cheese, grated
8 eggs
black pepper to taste, freshly ground
a handful of fresh savory, finely chopped
a pinch of dried marjoram
4 tablespoons wholemeal breadcrumbs

1. Strip the leaves away from the stalks, keeping the stalks for vegetable stock. Wash each leaf well, rinse under running water and lightly shake. Break the leaves in two and place in a shallow saucepan using the water that clings to the leaves after washing. On moderate heat, cook the leaves by turning them over frequently until the bulk is reduced and the leaves are heated through.

2. Heat 1 tablespoon olive oil in a small frying pan, add the onion and sauté gently over low heat for 5 minutes.

3. Meanwhile, beat the eggs with a whisk and add black pepper, savory and marjoram, mixing well. Stir in the cooked leaf beet and onion.

4. Heat the rest of the olive oil in a medium frying pan, until quite hot. Pour in half of the egg mixture (keeping half for the second omelette), tilting the pan to spread the batter evenly. Lift up the edges with a spatula and let the eggs spill over into the pan until well spread.

5. Sprinkle half the grated cheese over the top, cook for a minute or so, until slightly firm. Then sprinkle half the breadcrumbs over the cheese, cook for 1 minute.

6. Turn the omelette over and cook until golden brown on the underside. Repeat instructions 4-6 for the next omelette. Serve either immediately while hot, or later when cooled.

Wendy's Baked Stuffed Marrow

An exceptional vegetable stuffing, perfectly complementing the mild taste of the marrow container.

Serves 4
4 small-medium marrows (1 per person)
250g (8oz) garden peas, shelled
24 fresh basil leaves, finely chopped
250g (8oz) cous-cous
black pepper to taste, freshly ground
2 tablespoons butter
2 tablespoons lemon juice
250g (8oz) mushrooms, sliced
240ml (8fl.oz) water, boiled
a little olive oil

1. Pre-heat the oven to 180°C, 350°F, gas mark 4. Wash the marrows, cut off the top end of each and keep aside. Then cut each in half lengthways. Scoop out the seeds and discard them.

2. Place the cous-cous in a medium mixing bowl. Boil the water and pour over the cous-cous and leave it to swell, 2 to 3 minutes. Season with black pepper and stir in the butter until melted. Add in the sliced mushrooms, peas, lemon juice and chopped basil. Mix well.

3. Hold each marrow closed with one hand, or with cocktail sticks, and fill each with a quarter of the cous-cous mixture, pressing down the filling firmly. Replace the top ends and brush the outsides of the whole marrow with some olive oil.

4. Wrap the marrows firmly with aluminium foil and bake until tender, 40 to 50 minutes. Serve immediately while hot.

Pea Risotto

A fragrant rice dish best served with a cool salad.

Serves 4
125g (4oz) garden peas, shelled
250g (8oz) basmati rice
60g (2oz) butter
2 tablespoons shallots (2 small shallots), finely sliced
1 tablespoon dried mint
2 sprigs fresh rosemary
black pepper to taste, freshly ground
1.2litres (2pints) vegetable stock

1. Melt the butter in a large, deep saucepan and sauté the shallots over low heat until soft, 5 minutes, stirring constantly.

2. Wash and drain the rice. Add to the shallots in the saucepan, mixing well until the uncooked rice is coated with butter and shallots. Add the vegetable stock to the pan and turn up to high heat, stirring well. Bring this to the boil.

3. When the mixture has come to the boil, immediately lower the heat and let simmer. Add the peas, herbs and black pepper. Stir well and cover. Simmer over low heat until all the liquid has been absorbed and the rice is soft, 15 to 20 minutes. Check occasionally if water needs to be added.

4. Remove the herb sprigs and serve immediately while hot.

Peppers and Pasta (with Pesto)

A beautifully simple sauce to have with pasta.

Serves 4
1 pepper of each colour: red, green, yellow and orange
1 tablespoon olive oil
60g (2oz) pinenut kernels
1 medium onion, sliced
Italian Garden Pesto (see page 71)
black pepper to taste, freshly ground
2 teaspoons ground coriander
375g (12oz) pasta such as tagliatelle

1. Boil the pasta and drain. Keep hot in a heated saucepan.

2. Meanwhile, cut each pepper into quarters and remove the internal membranes and discard the seeds. Place the quarters with skin-side up on a tray under the grill. Grill the skin until it blackens and blisters. Remove from the grill and peel the skin away then cut them into long, thin strips.

3. Heat the oil in a frying pan on low heat. Add the onion and sauté until translucent, about 5 minutes. Add the coriander and black pepper and fry for another 3 minutes, stirring constantly. Add the peeled pepper strips and a little water to prevent burning. Stir the mix together well and heat through thoroughly.

4. Toss the pesto sauce through the hot, cooked pasta so it is well coated.

5. To serve, layer the heated pepper sauce over the pesto-pasta on warmed serving plates and sprinkle with the pinenut kernels. Serve hot.

Spinach Lasagne

In one word: scrumptious.

Serves 4

750g (1½ lb) spinach leaves
1 onion, chopped
125g (4oz) mushrooms, sliced
1 tablespoon olive oil
½ teaspoon of each: dried oregano, sage and thyme
125g (4oz) feta cheese
125g (4oz) cottage cheese
9 sheets precooked egg lasagne
for the topping:
30g (1oz) butter
1 tablespoon wholemeal flour
240ml (8fl.oz) milk, lowfat if preferred
90g (3oz) emmenthal cheese, grated
black pepper to taste, freshly ground
1 teaspoon ground nutmeg

1. Pre-heat the oven to 190°C, 375°F, gas mark 5. Oil a casserole or oven dish.

2. Wash the spinach leaves well, changing the water at least once. Heat a large saucepan and put in the spinach with the water that clings to the leaves after washing. Cook until just wilted, about 3 minutes, turning constantly. Remove from the heat and drain the water by pressing into a sieve.

3. Heat the oil in a frying pan and add the onion, sauté until soft, 3 to 4 minutes. Add the mushrooms and cook another 5 minutes. Remove from the heat. Add the spinach, oregano, sage and thyme to the pan, mixing together well.

5. In a small bowl, mix and break the feta and cottage cheeses together.

6. Arrange the layers as follows: half the spinach at the bottom; then 3 sheets of lasagne; next spread all the feta and cottage cheese mix; another 3 sheets of lasagne; the remaining half of spinach; finally the last 3 sheets of lasagne.

7. Prepare the topping by melting the butter in a small saucepan. Stir in the flour and remove from the heat and stir in the milk. Return to the heat until thickened, stirring constantly, 10 to 15 minutes. Add the emmenthal cheese, black pepper and nutmeg, mixing well. Then pour the topping evenly over the last lasagne layer.

8. Bake until the pasta sheets are cooked, 30 to 35 minutes.

Just Add a Little (Purées and Sauces)

Broad Bean Purée with Garlic

Serves 4
2kg (4lb) broad beans
boiling water
90g (3oz) butter
120ml (4fl.oz) vegetable stock
1 clove garlic, finely chopped
black pepper to taste, freshly ground
1/8 teaspoon ground nutmeg

1. Shell the beans and if necessary, remove the tough outer skin of each bean with a small sharp knife.

2. Place the beans into some boiling water, with the vegetable stock. Cook until tender, about 10 minutes. Drain and keep the cooking water aside.

3. Place the beans and garlic in a blender. Add 1 to 2 tablespoons of the cooking mixture and blend until a smooth consistency is achieved.

4. Return the purée to the pan, add the butter and cook over very low heat until very hot, about 5 minutes. Stir constantly. Just before serving, season with black pepper and the nutmeg.

Spicy Cucumber Yoghurt

A cross between the classic Greek *tzatziki* and the Indian *raita*, this aromatic dip is a useful palate cooler for a hot, spicy curry.

Serves 4-6
2 small cucumbers, or 1/2 long English cucumber, finely grated
4 tablespoons natural yoghurt, lowfat if preferred
1 clove garlic, finely chopped

some salt
1/4 teaspoon cumin seeds
1/4 teaspoon fennel seeds
a pinch of cayenne pepper
black pepper to taste, freshly ground
1 tablespoon fresh mint, finely chopped

1. Peel the cucumber and grate finely. Put this in a bowl, sprinkle with salt to draw out the moisture and place a heavy plate on top. After 10 minutes, remove the plate and drain the cucumber well.

2. Mix together the remaining ingredients, add the cucumber and mix well. Chill before serving.

Italian Garden Pesto

This very simple basil sauce (heavily laden with garlic) is perfect for tossing into thick strips of freshly cooked pasta, such as *fettucine* or *tagliatelle*, and serving hot. It is imperative to use *fresh* basil leaves in this recipe.

Serves 8-10
125g (4oz) fresh basil leaves
4-6 cloves garlic
60g (2oz) parmesan cheese, grated
4-6 tablespoons olive oil
60g (2oz) pinenut kernels

1. Peel the garlic. Wash the basil leaves and dry with paper towels or a cloth.

2. Purée all the ingredients in a blender. If the sauce is a little thick, then add more olive oil and blend again.

3. Use immediately or store in a tightly lidded container for later use.

Onion and Garlic Purée

A potent sauce for onion and garlic lovers. It combines well with leafy green vegetables such as kale, spinach and leaf beet.

Serves 4-6
375g (12oz) onions, chopped
3 garlic bulb heads
8 tablespoons olive oil

1. Bring some water to the boil in a small saucepan. Separate the cloves of garlic and drop into the boiling water for 2 minutes. Retrieve the cloves and peel.

2. In a large frying pan, heat the olive oil and add the chopped onions and whole garlic cloves. Cover the pan and cook over low heat, stirring occasionally, until both the onion and garlic are tender, 30 to 40 minutes. Leave aside to cool slightly.

3. Purée the garlic and onion, with the cooking juices, in a blender until fairly smooth. Set aside and reheat when needed.

Shallots and White Wine Butter Sauce

This pungent sauce is ideal for serving with mild tasting vegetables like chicory or potatoes.

Serves 4
$1^1/_2$ tablespoons shallots (2 shallots), finely chopped
3 tablespoons dry white wine
120ml (4fl.oz) vegetable stock
125g (4oz) butter
1 tablespoon fresh parsley, finely chopped
1 sprig fresh thyme
ground white pepper to taste

1. In a small saucepan, combine the wine, shallots, sprig of thyme and vegetable stock. On medium heat, bring to a slow boil and cook uncovered until the liquid has reduced by about half, 10 to 15 minutes. Stir occasionally. Remove from the heat and take out the sprig of thyme.

2. Warm the butter to room temperature then beat it until creamy. Add a little at a time to the shallot-wine mixture, beating well after every addition. When all the butter is added, mix in the parsley and pepper to taste. Set aside and reheat as neccssary.

Spicy Tomato Sauce

This hot and spicy sauce is perfect for livening up all sorts of vegetable dishes.

Serves 6-8
6 medium tomatoes, chopped
6 cloves garlic, finely chopped
1 medium onion, finely chopped
2 teaspoons olive oil
240ml (8fl.oz) water
black pepper to taste, freshly ground
$1\frac{1}{2}$ teaspoons ground cumin
2 teaspoons chilli powder
$\frac{1}{2}$ teaspoon dried basil
1 tablespoon fresh coriander, finely chopped

1. Prepare the tomatoes as follows: cut out the cores and immerse in simmering water for 30 seconds by which time the skin will be starting to peel away. Lift out of the water, peel and cut them in half. Squeeze out as many seeds as you can and chop up the remaining flesh.

2. Heat the oil in a medium saucepan, add the onion and sauté over medium heat until soft, 5 minutes. Add the cumin and chilli powder and cook another 5 minutes, stirring constantly.

3. Add the tomatoes and water to the saucepan, bring to the boil then simmer partially covered for 20 minutes. Add the garlic, black pepper and basil, stir well then simmer for another 10 to 15 minutes.

4. Add the coriander and process in a blender briefly, until fairly smooth but still a little chunky. Keep in a lidded jar in the refrigerator until required.

Desserts, Pies, Puddings and Cakes

Orchard Apple Tart

This one looks really impressive as well as tasting delicious.

Serves 6-8
3 medium cooking apples, Granny Smith or Bramley
90g (3oz) butter
125g (4oz) caster sugar
90g (3oz) ground almonds
30g (1oz) white flour
1 egg
1/2 teaspoon almond essence
2 tablespoons lemon juice
for the pastry:
170g (6oz) white flour
30g (1oz) icing sugar
125g (4oz) butter
2 tablespoons water

1. Pre-heat the oven to 200°C, 400°F, gas mark 6.

2. Prepare the pastry by firstly sifting the flour and icing sugar into a bowl. Rub in the butter by hand, until the mixture is crumbly. Make a hole in the mixture and fold in the water gradually until the batter becomes doughy but not sticky. Knead into a ball, wrap in foil or plastic film and chill for 30 minutes.

3. Butter a standard flan dish. Roll out the pastry and line the dish, including the edges. Cover the bottom with aluminium foil and a weight such as dried beans. Bake the pastry like this for 15 minutes. Reduce the oven to 180°C, 350°F, gas mark 4.

4. Prepare the filling: mix together the butter and sugar until smooth. Add the ground almonds, essence and flour, beating well. Pour this mix into the pastry lining.

5. Peel the apples and slice them into fairly thick slivers. Dip each slice into the lemon juice. Then arrange them carefully on top of the filling, like a spread set of playing cards with each slice slightly overlapping the next. Bake until golden, 25 to 30 minutes. Serve hot, warm or cooled.

Apple Muffins

These are best eaten straight out of the oven (but are still good the next day). Try slicing them in half and spreading with butter.

Makes 12 muffins

1 medium cooking apple, Granny Smith or Bramley, grated
75g ($2\frac{1}{2}$ oz) wholemeal self-raising flour
75g ($2\frac{1}{2}$ oz) white self-raising flour
90g (3oz) porridge oats
60g (2oz) brown sugar
60g (2oz) butter
$\frac{1}{4}$ teaspoon ground cinnamon
$\frac{1}{4}$ teaspoon ground nutmeg
2 eggs
180ml (6fl.oz) apple juice

1. Pre-heat the oven to 190°C, 375°F, gas mark 5.

2. Sift the flours and spices into a bowl. Rub in the butter by hand until it is crumbly. Stir in the oats and the sugar.

3. Lightly beat the eggs with a fork. Wash the apple and coarsely grate it without peeling.

4. In a separate bowl, make a hole in the centre of the flour mixture then gently fold in the apple juice and beaten eggs. Fold in the grated apple. The batter should be quite moist.

5. Butter 12 muffin pans. Spoon the batter in evenly and bake until golden brown, 20 minutes.

Ann's Apricot Flummerie

A deliciously light and fluffy dessert with just a touch of sweetness.

Serves 4
375g (12oz) fresh apricots
360ml (12fl.oz) evaporated milk
juice of one lemon
1½ tablespoons honey
1½ tablespoons agar-agar, or similar jelling compound
150ml (5fl.oz) whipping cream
boiling water

1. Remove the apricot stones and place the apricots in a saucepan with just enough water to cover. Bring to the boil, then simmer uncovered until the apricots are tender, 10 to 15 minutes. Let cool slightly then purée in a blender.

2. Put half the apricot purée into a small bowl, then put the bowl into a pan of boiling water reaching half way up the bowl. Dissolve the agar-agar into the apricots, then add the lemon juice. Stir in the honey until melted.

3. Pour the evaporated milk into a blender and gradually add the apricot-honey mixture, mixing gently. Add the remaining apricot purée until combined well. Pour into a serving bowl and refrigerate.

4. Just prior to serving, beat the cream and decorate the top of the dish.

Apricots with Almond Filling

The slightly grainy texture of the almond paste contrasts well with the smooth apricot flesh. Adjust the amount of sugar according to your taste and how sweet the apricots happen to be.

Serves 4-6
20 fresh apricots
juice of $\frac{1}{2}$ lemon
250g (8oz) white sugar
2 tablespoons water
for the filling:
100g (3$\frac{1}{2}$oz) ground almonds
60g (2oz) white sugar
1-2 tablespoons water
$\frac{1}{2}$ teaspoon vanilla essence

1. Remove the stones from the apricots carefully, keeping the fruit whole. Put the apricots in a medium saucepan with the lemon juice, 250g (8oz) sugar and water. Simmer covered until tender, 10 to 15 minutes. Leave to cool slightly.

2. Meanwhile, prepare the filling by mixing together all the filling ingredients in a mixing bowl, forming a sticky paste.

3. Remove the apricots from their cooking juices and divide the paste, filling each apricot. Serve in a glass bowl and pour the remaining syrup over the apricots. Add some cream or ice-cream just before serving.

Jungle Banana Bread

This is meant to be lovely and moist due to the bananas, so don't worry if at first it appears undercooked. Try spreading the slices with butter – especially good when the bread is just out of the oven.

Makes 2 loaf pans
6-8 medium bananas, very soft and ripe, mashed
1 heaped teaspoon instant coffee powder or granules
240ml (8fl.oz) boiling water
1 teaspoon orange zest (1 orange), grated
30g (1oz) poppy seeds
260g (8 1/2 oz) butter
200g (7oz) brown sugar
4 eggs
2 1/2 teaspoons vanilla essence
1/2 teaspoon almond essence
625g (1 1/4 lb) white flour
1 teaspoon salt
1/2 teaspoon bicarbonate of soda
1 tablespoon baking powder
1/2 teaspoon nutmeg
2 teaspoons cinnamon powder

1. Peel the bananas and mash with a fork or purée them in a blender. Combine the boiling water and coffee, then pour over the mashed bananas and leave to soak.

2. Butter 2 standard loaf pans. Sprinkle in the poppy seeds, shaking them all around to stick to the buttered pan. Pre-heat the oven to 180°C, 350°F, gas mark 4.

3. Beat the sugar and butter together until well mixed. Add the eggs gradually, beating well after each one. Then mix in the vanilla and almond essence, and orange zest.

4. Sift the flour, salt, soda, baking powder, cinnamon and nutmeg. Fold this into the sugar-butter mix, alternating with the bananas until everything is just mixed.

5. Pour the batter into the loaf pans and cook 50 to 60 minutes, or until a skewer comes out clean when poked into the centre.

6. Once cooked, leave to cool slightly and place on a cooling rack.

Real Banana Milkshake

A more simple recipe could not exist. Have it for breakfast, an afternoon or midnight snack.

Serves 2
1 very ripe banana
600ml (1 pint) milk, any type

1. Peel and slice the banana then put both ingredients into a blender and mix until smooth. Serve immediately.

Blackberry Sauce

This is an elegantly simple way of using up surplus berry pickings over the season. Serve this sauce over vanilla ice-cream, with Cornish clotted cream or over dollops of natural yoghurt.

Serves 4
250g (8oz) fresh blackberries
1-2 tablespoons white sugar
juice of 1/2 lemon

1. Place all the ingredients into a blender and purée until smooth.

2. Push through a strainer and discard the seeds. Adjust the amounts of sugar and lemon juice to taste. Store in a lidded container in the refrigerator and use when required.

Blackberry and Raspberry Pudding

These berries may easily be used interchangeably: simply swap the berries around.

Serves 6
250g (8oz) fresh raspberries (2 punnets)
250g (8oz) fresh blackberries
2-3 tablespoons caster sugar
1½ tablespoons cornflour

1. Place the raspberries and sugar in a blender and purée until smooth. Taste to adjust the amount of sugar if necessary.

2. Put the cornflour in a small saucepan and add the puréed berries, whisking constantly. Bring to a boil then simmer until slightly thickened, about 5 minutes, whisking constantly.

3. Place the whole blackberries into 6 glass serving bowls. Pour the raspberry sauce over the blackberries and chill before serving. Serve with cream or vanilla ice-cream.

Carrot Cake

Wonderfully moist, this cake will keep for a few days in the refrigerator (if there's any left after the first cut!)

Makes 1 loaf pan

250g (8oz) carrots, finely shredded
4 tablespoons lemon juice (1 lemon)
1 teaspoon lemon zest (1 lemon), grated
100g (3½oz) walnuts, chopped
125g (4oz) butter
100g (3½oz) brown sugar
2 eggs
1½ teaspoons vanilla essence
345g (11oz) white flour
½ teaspoon salt
¼ teaspoon bicarbonate of soda
1½ teaspoons baking powder
1 teaspoon cinnamon powder

for the icing:
250g (8oz) cream cheese
1 tablespoon natural yoghurt, lowfat if preferred
2½-3 tablespoons liquid honey

1. Wash and scrub the carrots. Shred finely and soak them in the lemon juice.

2. Butter a standard loaf pan. Pre-heat the oven to 180°C, 350°F, gas mark 4.

3. Beat the sugar and butter until they are well mixed. Add the eggs gradually, beating well after each one, then mix in the vanilla essence and lemon zest.

4. Sift the flour, salt, soda, baking powder and cinnamon. Fold these dry ingredients by hand into the sugar-butter mix, alternating with the carrots until everything is well mixed. Add the chopped walnuts and lightly fold into the mix.

5. Pour the mixture into the loaf pan and cook 50 to 60 minutes, or until a skewer comes out clean when poked into the centre. Once cooked, leave to cool slightly and place on a cooling rack.

6. Meanwhile, prepare the icing: blend all the icing ingredients together until smooth.

7. When the cake is cool, spread the icing evenly over the top and serve sliced.

Courgette Cake

The mild flavour of courgette combined with the nutty pinenut kernels gives this cake an unexpected yet delicious flavour and texture.

Makes 1 loaf pan
300g (10oz) courgette (2 small courgettes)
125g (4oz) butter
4 eggs
100g (3½oz) pinenut kernels
½ teaspoon caraway seeds
125g (4oz) brown sugar
300g (10oz) white flour
1 teaspoon salt
1½ teaspoons baking powder
1 teaspoon vanilla essence

1. Peel the courgettes and grate them coarsely. Pre-heat the oven to 220°C, 425°F, gas mark 7.

2. Blend the sugar and butter. Add the eggs one by one, mixing well after each one. Add the vanilla essence and mix.

3. In a bowl, sift the dry ingredients (except the pinenut kernels).

4. Fold the dry ingredients and the grated courgettes into the butter mixture, alternating between the two until well mixed. Lastly, fold in the pinenut kernels.

5. Butter a standard loaf pan and pour the batter in evenly. Smooth the top and sprinkle with the caraway seeds.

6. Bake for 10 minutes on high heat then turn the oven down to 180°C, 350°F, gas mark 4. Bake for another 45 to 55 minutes until a skewer comes out clean when poked into the centre.

7. Leave to cool slightly in pan, then knock out onto a cooling rack. Slice and serve.

Red and White Currant Pie

Depending on how sweet your tooth is, you may vary the amount of sugar mixed with the currants.

Serves 6-8
500g (1 lb) mixed white and red currants
170g (6oz) white sugar
for the pastry:
500g (1lb) white flour
1 teaspoon salt
250g (8oz) butter
4-5 tablespoons iced water

1. Butter a 20cm (8in) pie dish. Pre-heat the oven to 200°C, 400°F, gas mark 6.

2. Sift the flour and salt into a bowl. Place in a blender or mix in the butter and water gradually by hand until it rolls into a ball. Knead a little and wrap in foil or plastic film and chill for 30 minutes.

3. Roll out half the pastry and line the bottom and sides of the pie dish. Cover the base with foil and weights such as dried beans. Bake until cooked, 15 to 20 minutes.

4. Meanwhile, wash and drain the currants, removing their stalks. Then mix together the currants and sugar well. Pour into the pastry case. Roll out the remaining pastry and cover the berries evenly. Bake until golden brown, 25 minutes. Serve hot or cold, or freeze and reheat later.

Figs and Berry Cream

An unusually delightful combination. You can use either blackberries or raspberries for the berry cream.

Serves 4
8 fresh figs
125g (4oz) fresh raspberries (1 punnet), or blackberries
1 tablespoon caster sugar
300ml (10fl.oz) double cream

1. Wash the figs and cut them in half.

2. Wash and drain the berries then push them through a sieve and discard the seeds. Whip the cream until thick and stir the berries and sugar into the cream until well mixed.

3. Place large dollops of berry cream over each fig half and serve chilled.

Heligan Fruit Salad

This particular combination of fruits and freshly squeezed fruit juices turns an everyday fruit salad into something fantastic. Allow yourself at least four hours for chilling before serving.

Serves 4-6
4 blood plums, ripe, or any dessert plum
170g (6oz) seedless green grapes
2 nectarines, ripe
1 banana, not too ripe
360ml (12fl.oz) orange juice, freshly squeezed
3 tablespoons lemon juice, freshly squeezed
1 lemon zest, grated
30g (1oz) white sugar

1. Place the orange and lemon juices and grated lemon zest into a medium serving bowl.

2. Peel the nectarines, remove the stones and slice. Immediately put them into the fruit juice mix.

3. Wash the plums, remove the stones and slice. Add these to the fruit juice straight away.

4. Wash the grapes, remove them from their stalks and add to the fruit bowl.

5. Peel and slice the banana, again add to the fruit juices immediately.

6. Finally, sprinkle in the sugar and mix all the ingredients well. Cover and chill for at least 4 hours before serving and stir occasionally during this time. Serve with an optional topping of whipped double cream or natural yoghurt.

Kim's Gooseberry and Apple Pie

Serves 6-8
500g (1lb) fresh gooseberries
170g (6oz) white sugar
1 cooking apple, Granny Smith or Bramley, grated
for the pastry:
500g (1lb) white flour
1 teaspoon salt
250g (8oz) butter
4-5 tablespoons iced water

1. Butter a 20cm (8in) pie dish. Pre-heat the oven to 200°C, 400°F, gas mark 6.

2. Sift the flour and salt into a bowl. Place in a blender or mix in the butter and water gradually by hand until it rolls into a ball. Knead a little and wrap in foil or plastic film and chill for 30 minutes.

3. Roll out half the pastry and line the bottom and sides of the pie dish. Cover the base with foil and weights such as dried beans. Bake until cooked, 15 to 20 minutes.

4. Meanwhile, grate the apple without peeling and wash, drain and remove stalk ends of the gooseberries. Then mix together the gooseberries, grated apple and sugar. Pour this mixture into the pastry case.

5. Roll out the remaining pastry and cover the berries evenly. Bake until golden brown, 25 minutes. Serve hot or cold, or freeze and reheat later.

Gooseberry Fool

Cream and berries combined in this way are truly delicious every time.

Serves 4-6
500g (1lb) fresh gooseberries
170g (6oz) caster sugar
300ml (10fl.oz) double cream

1. Wash and drain the gooseberries, then remove any stalk ends. Place them in a medium saucepan and let them simmer in their own juices, without any added water. Simmer until tender, about 15 minutes. Leave them to cool slightly.

2. Place the cooled gooseberries in a blender with the sugar and purée until smooth.

3. Beat the cream until thick, then fold in the gooseberries. Place into individual glass serving bowls and refrigerate before serving.

Grapes with Orange Sauce

Due to its yoghurt base, this orange sauce has a wonderfully tangy overtone which could be a drink in its own right.

Serves 6
400g (13oz) fresh seedless grapes, green
800ml (1¼ pints) orange juice, freshly squeezed
1-2 tablespoons lime juice
1-2 tablespoons liquid honey

1. Whisk together the orange juice, lime juice and honey until well combined. Then cover and refrigerate at least 10 minutes.

2. Meanwhile, wash the grapes, remove from the stalks and shake them dry. Divide them equally amongst 6 small glass serving bowls. Spoon the chilled orange sauce over the grapes in each bowl and serve.

Lemon Meringue Pie

No recipe book would be complete without a Lemon Meringue Pie. This particular recipe has just the right amount of 'tang' balanced with sweetness, and a glorious full lemon flavour.

Serves 6-8

2 teaspoons lemon zest (2 lemons), grated
8 tablespoons lemon juice (3-4 lemons)
6 egg yolks
6 egg whites
90g (3oz) cornflour
250g (8oz) white sugar
360ml (12fl.oz) boiling water

for the pastry:

250g (8oz) white flour
1 teaspoon salt
125g (4oz) butter
3 tablespoons iced water

1. Pre-heat the oven to 220°C, 425°F, gas mark 7. Butter a 20cm (8in) pie dish.

2. Prepare the pastry: sift the flour and salt into a bowl. Place in a blender or mix in the butter and water gradually by hand until it rolls into a ball. Knead a little and wrap in foil or plastic film and chill for 30 minutes.

3. Roll out the dough and line the bottom and sides of the pie dish. Cover the base with foil and weights such as dried beans. Bake until cooked, 15 to 20 minutes. Reduce the oven to 150°C, 300°F, gas mark 2.

4. Meanwhile, in a medium saucepan over low heat add the cornflour and sugar. Stirring constantly, gradually add the boiling water. Bring to the boil, still over low heat, and stir constantly until the liquid has thickened slightly. Add the butter, mixing well.

5. Beat the egg yolks well and add them gradually to the saucepan. Continue to stir over low heat until well combined and thick. Add the lemon zest and juice, mix well. Set aside to cool slightly, then pour into the cooked pastry case.

6. Beat the egg whites until stiff and spoon on top of the lemon sauce in the pastry. Make sure the oven has reduced to the lower heat and bake slowly until the egg whites are light golden brown, 15 to 25 minutes. Serve hot, warm or cold.

Lemon Mousse

A light and fluffy mousse with lots of refreshing lemon tartness.

Serves 4-6
120ml (4fl.oz) lemon juice, freshly squeezed
1 teaspoon lemon zest (2 lemons), grated
2 egg whites
30g (1oz) cornflour
125g (4oz) white sugar
120ml (4fl.oz) water
300ml (10fl.oz) double cream

1. Wash and dry the lemons. Grate 1 teaspoon of zest, then squeeze the lemon juice.

2. In a small saucepan over medium heat add the cornflour and sugar, stirring constantly. Add the lemon juice and water and whisk vigorously until smooth.

3. Cook over low heat until the sauce has thickened, stirring constantly, 6 to 8 minutes. Remove from the heat and place into a mixing bowl. Stir in the lemon zest and set aside to cool to room temperature.

4. Beat the egg whites until stiff and then fold them into the lemon sauce, cover and refrigerate until well chilled, about 1 hour.

5. Whip the cream until thick, then fold this into the chilled lemon mixture. Cover and chill again for at least 10 minutes before serving.

Melon with Coconut

Two exotic flavours which combine perfectly together.

Serves 2-4
1 large melon, Honeydew or similar
1 coconut
juice of 1 lime
2-3 tablespoons liquid honey

1. Cut the melon in half, scoop out the seeds and discard them. Scoop out the flesh of each melon half with a large metal spoon, then cut these pieces into bite size bits. Use the empty melon halves as containers. Pile the chopped melon back into the hollowed out halves.

2. Extract the coconut milk by drilling 2 holes into the top. Keep this milk for later. Break open the coconut (with a hammer if you have to!) and free the flesh from its casing. Finely grate this flesh.

3. Now mix together the coconut flesh, coconut milk and honey. Spread this mixture evenly over the melon pieces and serve chilled.

Miss Tremayne's Melon Cup

Thick and fruity, this drink could be a meal in itself.

Serves 2-4
1 large melon, Honeydew or similar
1 small dessert apple
240ml (8fl.oz) water

1. Cut the melon in half and remove the seeds. Scoop out the flesh and place in a blender.

2. Peel and wash the apple, cut it into small pieces. Place the apple and water into the blender with the melon and blend all together until smooth. Serve chilled.

Nectarines in Syrup

Serves 4
4 ripe nectarines
250g (8oz) brown sugar
540ml (18fl.oz) water
juice and peel of 1 lemon

1. In a small saucepan over medium heat, add the water and peeled lemon rind. Add the sugar and stir until it is dissolved. Bring to the boil and cook for 3 to 4 minutes.

2. Peel the nectarines, remove their stones and slice thinly. Add the slices to the sugar syrup and simmer until the fruit is tender, about 5 to 6 minutes. Serve immediately while warm and top with vanilla ice-cream or whipped cream.

Nectarines in Brandy Cream

A brandy cream concoction, delicious in every way. Time is needed for chilling this dessert after preparation, so make it in the morning for the evening meal.

Serves 4
1kg (2lb) nectarines
1-2 teaspoons caster sugar
300ml (10fl.oz) double cream
3-4 tablespoons brandy
125g (4oz) brown sugar

1. Peel the nectarines, remove their stones and slice thinly. Place the slices in a very shallow ovenproof dish. Add the brandy and caster sugar.

2. Whip the cream until thick and spread it evenly over the top of the nectarine mix, forming a thickish layer.

3. Sprinkle the brown sugar evenly over the lot to form a thin icing (add more sugar if you prefer). Refrigerate for at least 8 hours, allowing the nectarines to be permeated by the brandy and sugar.

4. Just prior to serving, place the dish under a medium grill until the top forms a crunchy caramelised layer, 5 to 10 minutes (be careful not to melt the cream). Serve immediately.

Baked Orangey Custard

Deliciously light, filled with naturally sweet orange flavour.

Serves 4

2 teaspoons orange zest (2 oranges), grated
240ml (8fl.oz) orange juice, freshly squeezed
3 eggs
$3\frac{1}{2}$ tablespoons white sugar
240ml (8fl.oz) double cream

1. Pre-heat the oven to 180°C, 350°F, gas mark 4.

2. In a blender combine all the ingredients, starting with the eggs and gradually incorporating the rest. Blend until mixed thoroughly and smooth.

3. Divide the liquid evenly amongst 4 small glass ovenproof serving bowls. Place these bowls in a deep oven tray filled with boiling water that reaches halfway up. Bake until the custard is firm, 40 to 50 minutes. Serve hot, warm or cold.

Gingered Peaches

Especially for those who love fresh ginger – there's plenty of it!

Serves 4

4 large peaches, ripe
15g ($\frac{1}{2}$oz) fresh ginger root, finely chopped
280g (9oz) natural yoghurt, lowfat if preferred

1. Wash and dry the peaches. Remove their stones and slice them thinly. Place the slices into a small saucepan with just enough water to cover. Bring to the boil, then simmer uncovered until the peach slices are heated through, about 3 minutes.

2. Peel the ginger, finely chop it and mix with the yoghurt in a small mixing bowl.

3. Place the warm peach slices in small individual serving bowls and cover with the yoghurt-ginger topping. Serve immediately.

Baked Peachy Custard

With just a hint of maple syrup, the custard combines excellently well with the sliced peach base. You must endeavour to use *real* maple syrup.

Serves 6
2-3 large peaches
90ml (3fl.oz) real maple syrup
600ml (20fl.oz) milk, lowfat if preferred
4 eggs
1 teaspoon vanilla essence

1. Pre-heat the oven to 180°C, 350°F, gas mark 4.

2. In a blender, beat the eggs first, then add the vanilla essence, maple syrup and milk. Beat until well mixed and smooth.

3. Peel the peaches, remove their stones and slice them thinly. Distribute them evenly at the base of 6 small individual ovenproof glass bowls. Pour the maple-egg mixture evenly into each bowl. Place the bowls in a deep oven tray filled with boiling water which reaches halfway up each bowl.

4. Bake until the custard is firm, 40 to 50 minutes. Serve hot, warm or cold.

Spicy Pears in Red Wine Syrup

This is a variation of the traditional pears in red wine recipe where the added spices give a flavour reminiscent of Christmas mulled wine.

Serves 4-6
500g (1lb) pears, firm
300ml (10fl.oz) dry red wine
1 tablespoon cinnamon powder
$^1/_4$ teaspoon star anise, crushed
$^1/_4$ teaspoon ground nutmeg
5 whole cloves
$^1/_2$ teaspoon ground ginger
1 tablespoon liquid honey
90g (3oz) dates, chopped

1. In a medium saucepan over low heat, place the red wine and cinnamon. Stir until the cinnamon is dissolved. Add the honey, star anise, nutmeg and cloves, and bring to the boil. Simmer uncovered until all the ingredients are well dissolved and the liquid has reduced a little, stir constantly.

2. Peel the pears and cut them into quarters lengthways and remove the seeds and cores. Add these pear quarters to the liquid in the saucepan, over low heat. Chop the dates and add to the syrup. Stir frequently so the pears are well coated with the syrup and continue to simmer until the pears are tender, 15 to 20 minutes.

3. Serve the pears with the syrup while still warm and top with whipped cream or vanilla ice-cream.

Chocolate Pear Bake

Simple and quick to prepare, this dish has a lovely light and crunchy chocolate top (*real* chocolate is a must).

Serves 4-6
500g (1lb) pears, ripe
75g ($2^1/_2$oz) real dark chocolate
2 eggs
60g (2oz) caster sugar
60g (2oz) wholemeal flour
30g (1oz) flaked almonds
a little butter

1. Pre-heat the oven to 200°C, 400°F, gas mark 6. Butter a shallow oven dish about 25cm (10in) square.

2. Peel the pears and slice them thinly. Arrange them in the oven dish, distributed evenly.

3. Beat together the eggs and sugar in a blender or mixer until fluffy and light in colour.

4. Sift the flour into a mixing bowl. Gradually add the egg mixture into the flour and fold together lightly.

5. Melt the chocolate in a small saucepan or double boiler (in a bowl over a saucepan of boiling water). Gently fold the melted chocolate into the flour-egg mixture until well combined.

6. Pour the chocolate topping evenly over the pears and sprinkle with the flaked almonds. Bake until the topping is firm, 30 to 35 minutes. Serve hot, warm or cold with double cream or vanilla ice-cream.

Queen's Pineapple-Rum Bread Pudding

Good old-fashioned bread pudding given a new lease of life.

Serves 4-6
345g (11oz) fresh pineapple, after peeling and chopping
3 tablespoons rum, any sort
100g (3½oz) white bread
3 eggs
720ml (24fl.oz) milk, lowfat if preferred
2½ tablespoons white sugar
2 teaspoons vanilla essence

1. Pre-heat the oven to 180°C, 350°F, gas mark 4.

2. Cut the bread into cubes and spread evenly in a single layer in a shallow oven dish.

3. Cut the skin, base and leaves away from the pineapple. Slice fairly thinly, then carefully chop into small cubes, discarding the woody central core and any spiky bits. Retain as much juice as possible to add into the custard mixture below.

4. Beat together in a blender the rum, eggs, milk, sugar and vanilla essence until smooth. Add the pineapple pieces and juice to this custard and mix well.

5. Pour the custard over the bread chunks and bake until firm but moist, 20 to 30 minutes. Serve warm or cold with an optional topping of double cream.

Winch's Chilled Pineapple Cake

A delicious textural combination which needs no cooking, just a little time for chilling.

Serves 6-8
500g (1lb) fresh pineapple, after peeling and chopping
12 plain Digestive biscuits (or other sweet wholemeal-oatmeal biscuits)
100g (3 1/2 oz) butter
125g (4oz) icing sugar
2 egg yolks
300ml (10fl.oz) double cream

1. Beat together 60g (2oz) butter and the icing sugar in a blender or mixer until smooth and creamy. Add the egg yolks and beat again well. Transfer to a mixing bowl.

2. Cut the skin, base and leaves away from the pineapple. Slice fairly thinly, then chop into small cubes, discarding the woody central core and any spiky bits. Fold nearly all the pineapple chunks into the butter-egg mixture, keeping some aside for decoration.

3. Whip the cream until thick, then fold nearly all into the pineapple mixture, keeping some aside for decoration.

4. Melt the remaining butter in a small saucepan. Break up the biscuits until they resemble breadcrumbs and add to the melted butter in the pan, mixing thoroughly.

5. Butter a shallow glass serving dish, about 20cm (8in) diam. Make layers in the following order: one third of the biscuit crumbs at the bottom; next layer is half the pineapple-cream mixture; next is another third of the biscuit crumbs; again the remaining pineapple-cream mixture; lastly, top with the remaining third of biscuit crumbs.

6. Decorate with a few dobs of whipped cream and pineapple pieces. Cover and chill for several hours before serving.

Plum Pie Crumble

Gorgeously sweet Golden plums were used here, but any type of dessert plum will do.

Serves 6-8

for the filling:
1kg (2lb) ripe dessert plums
1-2 tablespoons brown sugar
3 tablespoons orange juice, freshly squeezed
3 tablespoons wholemeal flour
1 teaspoon cinnamon powder
a pinch of ground nutmeg

for the pastry:
150g (5oz) butter
225g (7½oz) white flour
3 tablespoons milk, lowfat if preferred

for the crumble:
170g (6oz) porridge oats
60g (2oz) wholemeal flour
½ teaspoon cinnamon powder
75g (2½oz) ground almonds
2 tablespoons brown sugar
3 tablespoons walnut oil

1. Pre-heat the oven to 200°C, 400°F, gas mark 6.

2. For the filling: wash, then remove the stones from the plums and slice them finely. Put them into a bowl and sprinkle with the sugar (vary the quantity, depending on the sweetness of the plums) and orange juice. Sift the flour, cinnamon and nutmeg together, then add to the plums and gently mix together.

3. Prepare the pastry: blend the flour and butter until crumbly. Add the milk gradually and mix with a wooden spoon until a smooth dough forms. Roll out the pastry. Butter a 20cm (8in) casserole or pie dish and line the base and sides with the pastry. Pour the plum filling, with all the juices, into the unbaked pastry.

4. Prepare the crumble topping: mix all the crumble ingredients together in a medium mixing bowl. Combine until all ingredients are well coated with the oil.

5. Spread the crumble topping evenly over the plum filling and press down firmly. Bake for 10 to 15 minutes (to cook the pastry), then reduce the oven to 190°C, 375°F, gas mark 5. Bake for another 25 to 30 minutes until golden brown. Serve hot, warm or cold with an optional topping of double cream or vanilla ice-cream (especially good when the pie is hot).

Samm's Raspberry Cream Pie

A superbly rich and creamy raspberry dessert with a crispy crunchy base.

Serves 6-8

for the base:
60g (2oz) butter
60g (2oz) brown sugar
170g (6oz) porridge oats
90g (3oz) wholemeal flour

for the filling:
375g (12oz) fresh raspberries (2½ punnets)

for the glaze:
185g (6½ oz) fresh raspberries (1½ punnets)
juice of ½ orange
2 tablespoons caster sugar
1 tablespoon cornflour
1 tablespoon water

for the topping:
300ml (10fl.oz) double cream
250g (8oz) natural yoghurt, lowfat if preferred
1 tablespoon liquid honey
juice of ½ orange
30g (1oz) toasted flaked almonds

1. Pre-heat the oven to 200°C, 400°F, gas mark 6. Butter a shallow ovenproof baking dish, 20 x 30cm (8 x 12in).

2. Prepare the base: put the flour and oats in a mixing bowl. Rub the butter into the mixture until it becomes crumbly. Mix in the sugar well.

3. Press this crumble mixture firmly into the oven dish, forming a thin layer, and bake until golden brown, 15 to 20 minutes. Remove from the oven and cool slightly. Break the cooked crumble into quite small bite size chunks. Arrange these crumble pieces in the base of a serving dish, 30cm (12in) diam.

4. Wash and shake dry the filling raspberries. Place nearly all of them evenly on top of the crumble chunks, keeping some aside for decoration.

5. Prepare the glaze: wash the remaining 1½ punnets of raspberries. Place them in a blender with the orange juice and caster sugar and purée until smooth (adjust the amount of sugar depending on the sweetness of the raspberries).

6. In a medium saucepan over low heat, add the cornflour and whisk in the puréed berries with the water. Continue to whisk while bringing to the boil, then simmer

until thickened, whisking constantly. Remove the glaze from the heat and set aside to cool. Then drizzle this glaze evenly over the fresh raspberries and crumble chunks.

7. Prepare the topping: whip the cream until thick and stiff. With a wooden spoon, stir in the yoghurt, honey and orange juice. Stir until well combined.

8. Pour the cream topping over the glazed raspberries and decorate with the toasted flaked almonds and remaining raspberries. Cover and refrigerate at least an hour before serving.

Rhubarb Fuggle

A delectable dessert, very creamy but not too sweet.

Serves 6
500g (1lb) fresh rhubarb stalks
60g (2oz) brown sugar
60g (2oz) butter
300ml (10fl.oz) double cream

1. Wash and trim the stalk ends of the rhubarb, pulling away any strings at the same time. Slice into quite large pieces.

2. Melt the butter in a medium saucepan over low heat, add the sugar and the rhubarb. Mix well until all the ingredients are combined.

3. Simmer, uncovered, over low heat until the rhubarb is cooked, about 10 minutes. Stir occasionally and the rhubarb will naturally break up and form a thick syrupy paste. Transfer to a bowl, let cool, then refrigerate until cool, about 20 minutes.

4. Meanwhile, whip the cream until thick but not too stiff. Once cool, fold the rhubarb gently into the cream. Pile the rhubarb cream into 6 tall glass goblets and serve chilled.

Summer Strawberries and Orange

More a combination suggestion rather than a formal recipe, these two fruits are ideal partners.

Serves 2-4
1 punnet fresh ripe strawberries
1 sweet orange, such as navel or blood
240ml (8fl.oz) orange juice, freshly squeezed
1-2 tablespoons white sugar (optional)

1. Wash and trim the strawberries, slicing them in half. Peel the orange and separate the sections, cutting each in half. Squeeze the orange juice, then place all these ingredients together in a serving bowl. Stir the whole lot together and chill for several hours before serving. If you prefer a slightly sweeter version, then add the sugar before chilling and stir until it dissolves into the orange juice.

Strawberry-Rhubarb Crumble

A simple and enticingly delicious combination.

Serves 6-8
1kg (2lb) fresh rhubarb stalks
600g (20oz) fresh strawberries
75g (2½oz) white sugar
for the crumble topping:
90g (3oz) porridge oats
135g (4½oz) wholemeal flour
1-2 tablespoons brown sugar
½ teaspoon cinnamon powder
a pinch of nutmeg
1 teaspoon orange zest, grated
125g (4oz) butter, melted

1. Pre-heat the oven to 190°C, 375°F, gas mark 5.

2. Wash and trim both the strawberries and rhubarb. Slice them up into bite size pieces and remove any rhubarb strings. Place all the fruit pieces in the bottom of a square 25cm (10in) oven dish. Sprinkle the white sugar evenly over the lot.

3. For the topping: melt the butter in a large saucepan. Sift together the flour, cinnamon and nutmeg. Add this to the butter along with the remaining topping ingredients. Mix together well.

4. Spread the crumble topping evenly over the fruit mix and press down firmly. Bake until crispy golden brown and the fruit is nicely boiling up around the sides, about 30 to 40 minutes. Serve hot, warm or cold with an optional dollop of cream or vanilla ice-cream.

Notes for Recipes

Salt

Salt has not been included in most of these recipes as vegetables contain plenty of naturally occurring salt minerals for flavour. If salt is required, sea salt or vegetable salt are probably the best alternatives and quantities may be added during cooking according to personal taste or presented on the table for the individual diner's use.

Butter

Conventional salted butter is used in the tested recipes. Margarine or soy substitutes can be used in place of butter and will work just as well.

Vegetable Stock

A pot of vegetable stock is easily prepared with just about any sort of vegetables, their peelings and lots of herbs and spices. The stock once made may be stored in a lidded jar in the refrigerator or kept frozen. Simple substitutes, such as vegetable stock cubes or pastes are easily available. Here is a basic recipe for some home-made vegetable stock:

500g vegetables and peelings, such as onion, leek, potato, celery and carrot
10 black peppercorns
2 sprigs fresh thyme
2 sprigs fresh rosemary
2 stalks fresh parsley
1 teaspoon dill seeds
2 bay leaves
1 lemon peel
750ml (25fl.oz) water

Place all the above ingredients in a large saucepan. Bring to the boil slowly, then simmer for 30 to 40 minutes. Strain out the liquid and store.

Herbs

Herbs' contribution to the flavour and aroma of the recipes within these pages is of paramount importance, so where possible, try to use fresh sprigs and leaves where specified. If it is impossible to obtain them fresh then dried herbs may be substituted: 1 teaspoon dried = 1 tablespoon fresh. Freezing fresh herbs in manageable amounts is a good way of storing them for long periods – just add them frozen, letting them defrost during cooking.

Heligan Vegetables

(with recipe references)

Asparagus

(Asparagus officinalis)

Originating in the Mediterranean and the Far East, wild asparagus was eaten as early as 200 B.C. in ancient Rome and Greece and has always been known for its efficacious medicinal qualities as a diuretic and laxative.

Young, thin spears of asparagus have a far superior flavour to older, thicker spears and are extremely delicious eaten raw when freshly picked. A handy hint for cooking them is to tie the spears in bunches, stand them vertically in some boiling water and let the tips steam until tender.

recipes

Cheesy Asparagus (see page 28)
Asparagus Grilled (see page 29)

Aubergine

(Solanum melongena)

Originally from warm, tropical areas of the world such as India and surrounding countries, aubergine is part of the Solanaceae family which includes tomato, bell pepper, tobacco and petunia. Aubergine is otherwise known as 'eggplant' in many parts of the world – a name taken directly from one of its more obscure varieties which is pure white in the shape of an egg.

Older, mature aubergines may need salting before cooking to draw out any bitterness, but fresh young ones can be added to your recipe without any special preparation.

recipes

Aubergines with Pesto (see page 30)
Aubergine Fritters (see page 31)

Beetroot

(Beta vulgaris)

Beetroot and leaf beet are inextricably linked through common ancestry and genetic ties. They are distinguished today by the purpose for which each is cultivated on a commercial scale. Nowadays, the beetroot's root and the leaf beet's leaf are of primary importance, but a little known fact is that not until the early eighteenth century was the beetroot's root eaten at all. Right through the ages up until the 1700's, the beetroot's leaf was the thing to be eaten and is well worth trying. In those days, it must have been called simply 'beet' or 'red beet' as it is alternatively known today. Suffering numerous developments and changes, the beetroot of today comes in all sorts of shapes and sizes, from long to globular spheres.

Try not to damage the skin when scrubbing the roots of beetroot as this will cause bleeding during cooking. Baking beetroot whole really entices out its natural sweetness – wrap it in foil and bake in a moderate oven for up to 3 hours.

recipe

Beetroot Salad with Chicory and Celery (see page 20)

Leaf Beet

(Beta vulgaris var. *cicla)*

Leaf beets are more generally known by their assorted varietal names such as Swiss chard, seakale beet, silver beet and spinach beet, all grown for distinct purposes – the chard varieties were originally developed only for their tasty midribs while spinach beet was fostered specifically for its leaves.

Nowadays, none of the leaf beet is wasted – leaves, stalks and midribs are quite happily consumed. Freshly picked immature leaves make superbly crisp salads while more mature leaf beets are delicious when steamed or boiled very briefly. When true spinach is unavailable, the leaf beets make a perfectly acceptable substitute.

recipes

Leaf Beet (Swiss chard) and Cheese Omelette (see page 64)
Leaf Beet (Swiss chard) and Onions (see page 46)

French Bean and Runner Bean

(Phaseolus vulgaris, P. coccineus)

Known under various names such as snap, string or green beans, the French and runner beans originally came from South America. Runner beans are generally larger, coarser and darker in colour than French beans but there is no discernible difference when it comes to cooking them.

Crisp young pods, picked straight from the bush, have no rivals for taste whether eaten completely raw and crunchy or cooked very quickly. There is only one rule to keep in mind with green beans – cook them for no more than five minutes to keep them crisp and for evermore dispel the illusion that beans are limp, tasteless and watery, reminiscent of school dinners best forgotten!

recipes

Green Beans with Almonds (see page 32)
Green Beans with Onion (see page 32)

Broad Bean

(Vicia faba major)

The broad bean has been a staple food of Mediterranean and European diets since ancient times and was occasionally awarded privileged status in societies such as ancient Rome where it was once venerated in traditional funeral feasts.

Although a favourite with home gardeners, the broad bean seems to be a much maligned vegetable in the kitchen. The most likely reason for this is that the majority of cooks are unaware of how to prepare a broad bean for cooking. The key to unlocking the fresh nutty flavour of these beans is simply to pick them when young. But if only older beans are to be found, then peel off the tough skin of each individual bean once slipped out of its pod – do this while listening to your favourite piece of music and you'll never regret it.

recipes

Buttered Bothy Beans (see page 33)
Broad Bean Purée with Garlic (see page 70)

Broccoli

(Brassica oleracea)

Broccoli and cauliflower both originate in Italy, have similar cultivation needs and possess the same botanical name, but the similarity ends there. Various types of broccoli exist in the world today, including green, purple or white sprouting, as well as the tightly packed green heads we are familiar with on the greengrocer's shelf, known also as 'calabrese'.

A beautifully decorative vegetable, the broccoli's form, texture and flavour must be kept intact by minimal cooking time or simply by eating it raw. Don't be surprised by the regal coloured water which drains away from the cooked purple sprouting form – that is purely a natural consequence of the cooking process.

recipes

Cream of Broccoli Soup (see page 10)
Broccoli and Pasta (see page 60)

Brussels Sprouts

(Brassica oleracea)

Supposedly from Belgium and grown abundantly around Brussels in the 1500's (as its name suggests), the Brussels sprout's exact origins are rather obscure.

Its reputation has been unduly tarnished by generations of overcooking, creating disastrously flavoured mush. The joyous, nutty and delicate flavour of sprouts is achieved only through quick boiling or steaming for a matter of minutes (no more than seven minutes boiled, and up to fifteen minutes steamed). The traditional cross sliced into the sprout's base quickens the cooking time, so keep an eye on the crispness factor if you opt for this cross-cutting technique.

recipes

Brussels Sprouts with Garlic (see page 34)
Brussels Sprouts and Chestnuts (see page 35)

Cabbage

(Brassica oleracea)

Cultivated since ancient times, the cabbage is said to have originated in the Mediterranean and surrounding areas.

Cabbages, whether red, green or white, crinkly or smooth, are always delightfully crisp and crunchy. Choose your varieties carefully according to your particular culinary needs at the time. For instance, green or white cabbage makes wonderful fermented sauerkraut or crispy coleslaw salad, while red cabbage is best suited to pickling and making a sweet and sour side dish.

recipes

Cabbage and Caraway Salad (see page 21)
Annabel's Red Cabbage (see page 36)

Cardoon

(Cynara cardunculus)

Originally from the Mediterranean, cardoons were extremely popular in Britain for centuries until they inexplicably fell out of favour around the late 1800's. Thankfully, they haven't been lost forever in the annals of time but appear to be experiencing a minor comeback.

The important part of the cardoon for eating is the stem, as opposed to the edible flowerhead of its close relative, the globe artichoke. If you can't easily obtain cardoons locally, then you could try growing them at home. Their flavour may be described as delicately subtle with a smooth and slightly crunchy texture. Counterbalance their subtle flavour with some non-subtle sauces such as hot chillies and garlic.

recipe

Cardoons with Garlic Butter (see page 37)

Carrot

(Daucus carota)

The original wild and tough carrot from Asia and the Middle East has been metamorphosed into the present day sweet domesticated form, cultivated since the fourth century B.C. Decorative in ornamental gardens as well as the kitchen garden, resourceful ladies of the early 1600's apparently used to adorn their hair with the carrot's 'prettily-tinted' autumn foliage.

Carrots are a well-known multi-purpose vegetable, especially delicious when picked young and early. Whether you peel them or not is entirely up to you but it would be wise to remove the peel from carrots not grown organically.

recipes

Carrot Soup with Ginger (see page 11)
Carrot Cake (see page 83)
Cucumber and Carrot Salad (see page 21)

Cauliflower

(Brassica oleracea)

Cauliflower and broccoli are closely related botanically, have similar cultivation needs and both originate in Italy. Cauliflower has been around for centuries in various forms and assorted nomenclature, such as Gerard's descriptive fifteenth century name of 'coleflowery'.

Most of us would recognise the magnificent coral-like white heads of cauliflower found abundantly across the country but there also exist some atypical varieties of a green hue and interesting conical shape. As with broccoli, all types of cauliflower florets are delicious raw, or should be cooked briefly to retain their lovely crisp texture and delicate flavour. There is a myriad of exciting ways to cook this vegetable, besides the ubiquitous cauliflower cheese, using richly flavoured sauces, herbs and spices.

recipes

Cauliflower and Ricotta Pie with Potato Crust (see page 61)
Spicy Cauliflower Casserole (see page 62)

Celeriac

(Apium graveolens var. *rapaceum)*

Of Mediterranean origin, this celery flavoured root was grown in Europe fairly late in the history of vegetable cultivation, during the seventeenth century. As its name suggests, celeriac is part of the celery fraternity with the difference being that the large globular root is consumed, as opposed to the stalks of celery.

The one great advantage of celeriac is that you get the wonderfully delicious flavour of celery permeating your recipes without the stringy fibres. Raw celeriac grated into salads is just as delectable as celeriac cooked. Due to its very nature, this root merges well in stews and roasts delightfully, without losing its lovely textural qualities.

recipe

Celeriac and Potato Pancake Cribs *(see page 63)*

Celery

(Apium graveolens var. *dulce)*

Descending from the wild inedible form of temperate Europe, celery has undergone many developments to become the sweet, delicately flavoured vegetable it is today.

The fibrous strings of the celery stalk are easily pulled away using a knife – this is preferable to pulling them out of one's teeth! Celery's crunchy fresh crispness is best appreciated raw in salads or filled with such things as peanut butter (ideal as a healthy snack), but cooking celery in various ways can be just as delicious.

recipes

Celery and Sunflower Seed Soup *(see page 12)*
Beetroot Salad with Chicory and Celery *(see page 20)*

Chicory

(Cichorium intybus)

A fortuitous accident in nineteenth century Brussels gave rise to the creamy-white leaves of chicory as we know it today. Initially, white shoots were discovered sprouting from some coffee making chicory roots that were left in the dark – this prompted further investigation and development of the light exclusion technique, 'blanching', employed today.

During the cold, dreary winter months, chicory blesses us with its fresh and bright presence. Uncooked leaves make lovely winter salads while whole baked or lightly boiled heads marry well with full flavoured aromatic sauces such as herb and cheese.

recipes

Baked Chicory with Herby Cheese Sauce (see page 38)
Beetroot Salad with Chicory and Celery (see page 20)

Courgette

(Cucurbita pepo)

We can only speculate as to the true origin of courgettes – they seem most likely to have come from ancient Persia across into Europe. They resemble baby marrows simply because that is what they are. Also known as 'zucchini' – derived from the golden coloured variety of the same name.

Deliciously mild with a nutty flavour and firm succulent flesh, the courgette should have a place in everyone's kitchen. Most people tend to cook this vegetable (one of many) for far too long – it's a tragedy to destroy the delicate flavour in this way. Grill, steam or bake courgettes and eat the young ones raw if you are so inclined, but do not ever boil courgettes as you won't recognise the wonderful vegetable you have just annihilated! You might like to experiment with stuffed courgette flowers on the side.

recipes

Grilled Courgettes with Parmesan (see page 39)
Courgette Cake (see page 84)

Cucumber

(Cucumis sativus)

Probably one of the oldest cultivated vegetables, cucumbers were granted a mention in the Old Testament and were once a great favourite of the Emperor Tiberius in Roman times who had them grown wherever he went. Many varieties are grown today including long, smooth forms; ridged forms; baby forms for pickling and seedless versions.

Oscar Wilde immortalised the cucumber sandwich as the epitome of high social graces in Victorian England, but fortunately for us today, the cucumber is no longer a luxury item. It is without doubt best to use fresh cucumbers with their peel intact, but if they have happened to stay in the refrigerator longer than anticipated, you can still make use of them by peeling away the aged skin. Cucumbers may be boiled, steamed or baked, but are really at their best untouched by the cooking process.

recipes

Cucumber and Carrot Salad (see page 21)
Spicy Cucumber Yoghurt (see page 70)

Fennel, Sweet

(Foeniculum vulgare var. *dulce)*

Native to the Mediterranean and naturalised in many parts of the world, Florence, French or sweet fennel has been used for culinary and medicinal purposes for centuries.

Whether one classifies it as herb, vegetable or both, there is no doubt that fennel should become a much more familiar culinary item than it is now. Besides the roots, all parts of the fennel plant are edible with a gorgeous aniseed flavour – the seeds, feathery leaves and bulbous leaf stalks. As a vegetable, the leaf stalks can be eaten raw or cooked in various ways such as boiling in vegetable stock for a few minutes and serving hot with a delicious cheese sauce.

recipes

Fennel Soup with Potato (see page 13)
Fennel Salad with Walnuts (see page 22)

Garlic

(Allium sativum)

There is no middle line (no sitting on the fence) with garlic – you either love it or hate it! Garlic is a blessing to all who cook as its presence in countless savoury dishes is essential for heightening the recipe's flavours. Attributed with folkloric properties for assuaging vampires and evil curses, garlic is also credited with innumerable healing qualities. Of Mediterranean and southern Asian origin, it has been cultivated since antiquity.

With just a little attention, you can easily manipulate garlic's power through the key factors of preparation and timing. For instance, crushing with a garlic press will create a far more pungent flavour than crushing with a mortar and pestle; finely chopped garlic provides a more potent flavouring than crushing, and burnt or browned cloves are rendered inedibly bitter. Control garlic's strength by timing – the later you add it to a dish, the stronger the flavour. A handy hint for peeling garlic cloves is to either drop them into boiling water for a couple of minutes or crush them firmly with a wide knife blade on its side, then pull away the separated skin.

recipes

Italian Garden Pesto (see page 71)
Peppers and Pasta (with Pesto) (see page 67)
Baked Garlic with Herb Cheese (see page 40)
Cardoons with Garlic Butter (see page 37)
Onion and Garlic Purée (see page 72)
Kale with Onion and Garlic Purée (see page 44)
Broad Bean Purée with Garlic (see page 70)

Globe Artichoke

(Cynara scolymus)

Originally from the western and central Mediterranean region, the globe artichoke was popularised in Britain during King Henry VIII's reign, purported to be one of his favourite vegetables and possessing aphrodisiac properties.

Globe artichokes are mostly cooked but you can eat the very young ones raw. To help prevent discolouration after cutting, use stainless steel utensils and dip the artichoke pieces into acidulated water (with lemon juice). Eating them is not entirely straightforward, but easy once you get the hang of it – simply remove each leaf from the globe and scrape it between your teeth, leaving all the fibrous bits behind, then eat the deliciously tender 'heart', but avoid the tiny spiky hairs which surround it.

recipes

Globe Artichokes and Mushrooms (see page 41)
Globe Artichokes with Asparagus and Green Olive Sauce (see page 42)

Jerusalem Artichoke

(Helianthus tuberosus)

The Jerusalem artichoke tuber is not related to globe artichoke in any other way than by its common name. Actually related to the sunflower and producing sunny yellow blooms, Jerusalem artichoke originates in North America and was supposedly brought to France from Canada in the early 1600's.

A truly delicious vegetable with a flavour all of its own, there's no need to peel the tubers if grown organically and they can even be eaten raw. To avoid toughening the skin when boiling, a good hint is to place the tubers into *cold* water initially then bring to the boil.

recipes

Cream of Jerusalem Artichoke Soup – The Head Gardener's Favourite (see page 14)
Jerusalem Artichokes tossed in Breadcrumbs (see page 43)

Kale (Borecole)

(Brassica oleracea var. *acephala)*

An ancient vegetable originally from the Mediterranean, numerous edible varieties of kale are grown these days as well as some inedible garishly coloured decorative forms for the ornamental garden.

Kale has a rather undeserved reputation for being tough and bitter, but this is far from the truth. A lovely rich green leaf vegetable, it partners well with spicy, potent sauces such as chilli, onion and garlic.

recipe

Kale with Onion and Garlic Purée (see page 44)

Kohlrabi

(Brassica oleracea var. *caulo-rapa)*

Kohlrabi's flavour closely resembles cabbage and its texture is like turnip which helps explain its German name (it's a Northern European native), translated as 'cabbage turnip'. Its rounded root-like appearance is deceptive since in actuality, kohlrabi is a hugely bloated stem.

As is the norm with most vegetables, the smallest, youngest ones have the best flavour, whether you are using purple or green varieties. You don't need to peel them unless the skin appears tough and leathery.

recipe

Kohlrabi, Cream and Spice (see page 45)

Leek

(Allium ampeloprasum)

Often referred to in ancient texts such as the Bible, the leek has been cultivated for at least 3000 years and most probably originated in the Mediterranean, with its popularity reaching a zenith in the Middle Ages. The thick stem, which is actually a bunch of tightly rolled leaves, is whitened ('blanched') during the growing process by excluding light.

Leeks are a welcome winter mainstay playing a major role in the modern European diet. Because of the way they are grown, the soil which is packed around the stem may be caught in between the leaves, so the best way to clean leeks is to slice them in half lengthways and rinse very thoroughly, making sure you loosen all the soil hidden away. Their mild oniony flavour makes them particularly valuable as a raw salad ingredient as well as a cooked general purpose seasoning.

recipes

Baked Leeks with Aromatics (see page 47)
Leek and Herby Cheese Ramekin Pies (see page 48)

Lettuce

(Lactuca sativa)

Originally found in the Mediterranean wild only as a loose-leaf form, the number of varieties cultivated today is staggering – including a wonderful choice of greens and reds; crispy solid firm heads and crinkly rounded forms. The ubiquitous lettuce has been popular throughout the ages, reputed to possess healing qualities as well as culinary pleasures.

A life without lettuce salads to supplement our modern day diet is hardly comprehensible. A couple of hints to bear in mind when preparing this leafy vegetable are to tear the leaves by hand rather than cutting them with a knife (this makes the leaf edges brown) and dress the leaves at the last minute to prevent sogginess.

recipes

Lettuce Salad with Sugarsnap Peas and Chilli (see page 23)
Lettuce Salad with Grapes and Cashews (see page 24)

Marrow

(Cucurbita pepo)

The pride and joy of many an amateur gardener, the marrow originally from South America has an almost infinite capacity to grow and grow. Because of this indomitable feature, it was extremely popular in early nineteenth century England and remains a favourite to this day.

Although the marrow's huge size is prized amongst gardeners, the opposite is true amongst culinary experts – that is, a smaller immature marrow has a far superior flavour to a large, somewhat watery one. The mild flavour of marrows is best complemented by fragrant herbs and spicy sauces, while the most common cooking method is to stuff this perfectly shaped container with a deliciously aromatic filling.

recipes

Wendy's Baked Stuffed Marrow (see page 65)
Herb-baked Marrow Chunks (see page 49)

Mushroom

(Agaricus bisporus, A. campestris, Pleurotus ostreatus)

A plethora of mushroom species exist in the world today, either cultivated by the millions or growing wild in field and forest. Some in the wild are poisonous and hallucinogenic, making mushroom hunting a rather exciting but risky pastime! The most common commercially grown types include button, field and oyster mushrooms, all of different species.

Mushrooms are wonderfully versatile, whether cooked or raw, as a complementary flavouring, or the primary component of a meal. The question of how to prepare a mushroom is rather a contentious one – some advocate peeling, others prefer washing with a damp cloth and yet others will run them under cold water. Basically, it is up to your own discretion, but do make sure they are thoroughly dried before adding them to your recipes. Button mushrooms (most commonly available) have the mildest flavour while the field and oyster varieties are quite richly flavoured with a coarse texture – they should be cooked separately to avoid unwanted colouring of accompanying ingredients. Mushroom storage is also an issue for debate, but suffice it to say that keeping them in a paper bag is a much better option than in a plastic one.

recipes

Baked Stuffed Mushrooms (see page 50)
Globe Artichokes and Mushrooms (see page 41)
Wendy's Baked Stuffed Marrow (see page 65)

Onion

(Allium cepa)

Originally from Asia, the onion is bestowed with luminary status, mentioned not only in the Old Testament as an Israelite luxury, but was an intrinsic component of the ancient Egyptian slaves' diets who built the Great Pyramids – perhaps then we should thank the humble onion for its involvement in this monumental achievement!

Both revered and reviled, the onion is undoubtedly a quintessential ingredient for a vast majority of dishes. Folklore abounds with methods to prevent tearful eyes during onion preparation and everyone has their own 'failsafe' technique – here's one to try: before peeling, put the onion in the freezer for ten to fifteen minutes, then peel and chop, without shedding a tear. Both flavour and odour can be controlled by carefully choosing specific varieties and through the preparation method – grated onion has a more potent flavour than sliced or chopped onion, and mild salad onion varieties are easily consumed raw.

recipes

Leaf Beet (Swiss chard) and Onions (see page 46)
Onion and Garlic Purée (see page 72)
Kale with Onion and Garlic Purée (see page 44)

Parsnip

(Pastinaca sativa)

Naturalised in Britain today, parsnip was originally the principle staple food of Europe (preceding the potato), reaching the heights of fame in Shakespeare's *Macbeth*. Due to its very distinctive flavour, parsnip was well suited to its traditional role in breadmaking and in flavouring wine and beer.

Endowed with a curiously sweet flavour all of its own, parsnip needs little dressing up or disguising – simply bake it with butter or fry it into chips and enjoy its mellow sweetness.

recipes

Parsnip and Potato Soup (see page 15)
Parsnip Fritters (see page 51)

Pea

(Pisum sativum)

Cultivated for aeons and originating in Western Asia and Central Europe, the pea has deservedly earned its place as one of the world's favourite leguminous vegetables. Many interesting and diverse forms are grown today including shelling garden varieties, field-grown split peas and mange-tout forms where pods and all are eaten.

The preparation of each pea varies according to type, but the common denominator with peas is the imperative to cook them quickly, if at all! (A possible exception is if you simply can't go without the British institution of 'mushy peas'.) All varieties of freshly picked peas, kept raw, are deliciously sweet and crisp, perfect for a salad.

recipes

Mange-tout Peas with Red Pepper (see page 52)
Pea Risotto (see page 66)
Lettuce Salad with Sugarsnap Peas and Chilli (see page 23)
Wendy's Baked Stuffed Marrow (see page 65)

Pepper

(Capsicum annuum)

Originally from the tropical regions of Central and South America, the peppers described here (not to be confused with fiery hot chilli peppers) are now cultivated the world over. Beautifully decorative in many shapes and colours, these wondrously delectable vegetables are widely known as sweet peppers due to their flavour; bell peppers due to their shape; and capsicum due to their botanical namesake.

Most peppers are green initially, changing colour quite spectacularly upon maturity – that is how red, yellow, orange and purple varieties are formed. If you need a bit of colour in your salad or pasta, then peppers are an excellent choice. Peeled peppers are not a necessity but try it once and you'd be surprised how much sweeter a skinless pepper can be. Simply cut a pepper into quarters, place under the grill skin-side up, wait until the skin blackens and blisters, then under cold running water, effortlessly rub away the skin.

recipes

Peppers and Pasta (with Pesto) (see page 67)
Mange-tout Peas with Red Pepper (see page 52)

Potato

(Solanum tuberosum)

Originally from the magnificent Andean highlands of Peru and Bolivia, potatoes have only become popular in other parts of the world relatively recently, since the sixteenth century. Even though world production on a grand scale now occurs in the northern hemisphere, the varieties of potato available in the western world are disappointingly few compared to the myriad of colours and shapes still found in South American markets.

Potatoes are used in every way imaginable in nearly every part of the world, available all year round wherever you look. Every spring we wait in anticipation for the arrival of glorious new potatoes – these less than mature varieties must be the crown prince of potatoes, deliciously sweet especially for boiling and salads. Mature potatoes are more starchy, making them more suitable to mashing and chip-making. Although most people tend not to peel new potatoes, most of us would automatically peel a mature potato, but the advice here is not to peel them either – unless you require a perfectly smooth purée or mash. Potato peel itself can be made into an enticing dish if you deep-fry it like chips and spice it up with a hot chilli sauce – most of the nutrition is held in the skin so this makes a healthy meal as well. Although we shouldn't eat sprouted potatoes, it is quite acceptable to cut away any green parts which don't actually affect the rest of the potato's digestibility.

recipes

Chunky Mashed Potatoes with Black Olives (see page 53)
New Season Potato Salad (see page 25)
Parsnip and Potato Soup (see page 15)
Fennel Soup with Potato (see page 13)
Turnip and Potato Soup (see page 17)
Celeriac and Potato Pancake Cribs (see page 63)
Cauliflower and Ricotta Pie with Potato Crust (see page 61)

Pumpkin and Squash

(Cucurbita maxima, C. pepo)

Famous as a hollowed out Halloween spook, pumpkin deserves much more attention than it presently receives in this country. Both pumpkin and squash have been crossed and interbred over the years, creating some confusion as to each's identity. However, whether a pumpkin is a squash or *vice versa*, makes no real difference in the cooking world – most varieties can be used interchangeably, depending on availability. Before European exploration, both pumpkin and squash were a staple food of the South American population, from where these vegetables originated.

The inherent sweetness of pumpkin and squash can be best appreciated by roasting unpeeled chunks in an oiled baking dish until they become succulently tender. Boiling or steaming peeled slices is quicker than roasting and can be just as delicious by combining with dollops of butter and the traditional complementary pumpkin spices of nutmeg and cinnamon.

recipe

Jen's Spicy Pumpkin Soup (see page 16)

Radish

(Raphanus sativus)

The crunchy pepper flavoured radish dates back to at least the Pharaohs' time in Egypt and an entire book was dedicated to them in ancient Greece, indicating their ancient popularity. Contrary to popular belief, radishes are not always pink, white and round – there are lots of different radish shapes, sizes and colours from round to long and red to purple.

Over-mature and stored radishes will have lost their crunch, tending towards woodiness and complete lack of flavour, so eat them as fresh as possible. Treat radishes with simplicity and respect – eat them raw with an uncomplicated salad dressing or simmer briefly in some vegetable stock and butter – nothing more is needed.

recipe

Radish Salad (see page 26)

Scorzonera and Salsify

(Scorzonera hispanica, Tragopogon porrifolius)

Not a particularly familiar sight in British kitchens, scorzonera and salsify roots have been traditionally collected wild in the Mediterranean for centuries and been cultivated in Europe since the sixteenth century. Salsify with its oyster-like flavour, hence its alternative name of 'oyster vegetable', is perhaps more commonly known than its close sooty skinned cousin, scorzonera.

Both of these rather nutty flavoured root vegetables are often grown interchangeably according to season and demand, therefore may be unwittingly substituted at the green-grocers without warning. Flexibility is an easy virtue in this case, as one switched for the other during cooking makes no discernible difference. When chopping these roots, place them in acidulated water (with lemon juice) to prevent discolouration.

recipes

Scorzonera in Cheese Sauce (see page 54)
Fried Salsify (see page 55)

Shallot

(Allium ascalonicum)

Shallots are a dual purpose vegetable where both the luscious spring onion-like leaf tops and the subtly smooth flavoured onion-like bulbs are utilised. Originating in eastern Mediterranean countries, shallots have been a favourite of European gourmets since at least the ninth century.

Their delicate sophisticated flavour has been best exploited in modern times by the French who recognise the shallot's valuable contribution to sauces, purées and dressings. The shallot bulb can be easily substituted for onion in most cases and the green leaf shoots swapped for spring onion if creative improvisation is called for.

recipes

Shallots and White Wine Butter Sauce (see page 73)
Roast Shallots (see page 55)

Spinach

(Spinacia oleracea)

Popeye sung the praises of strength-enhancing spinach for good reason. As any nutrition expert will tell us, this marvellously rich green leafy vegetable has plenty of vitamins and minerals to keep us fit and healthy. Originally from Persia, the wise Chinese recognised spinach's worth in the seventh century from where it spread into Europe around the twelfth century.

Aside from feeling virtuous while eating it, spinach is a real pleasure for the taste buds, especially when combined with garlic and a mixture of soft cheeses such as cottage and ricotta. Spinach is at its indisputable best when picked straight from the garden into the frying pan, but in the real world, leaves will keep quite well covered in plastic in the refrigerator at least a couple of days. Inevitably, soil and grit will accompany a bunch of spinach (unless hydroponically grown) so rinse and rinse again until no traces of grit are left. Delicately flavoured baby leaves left whole make scrumptious salads.

recipes

Spinach Lasagne (see page 68)
Spinach and Pinenut Kernels (see page 56)

Spring Onion

(Allium fistulosum)

Of Asian origin, spring onions were a late arrival into European cuisine around the early eighteenth century. Specifically cultivated for their pungent stems and leaves, these onion varieties are also known as scallions, bunching or salad onions.

There is nothing complicated about preparing spring onions – simply wash and slice, then add them at the last minute to salads, dips or stir-fries or eat them whole either grilled or raw.

recipe

Grilled Spring Onions (see page 56)

Swede

(Brassica napus)

A legacy of eastern European time-honoured farming traditions, the swede is now a staple crop in central and northern European communities. Often confused with turnips due to their similarity in appearance and growing requirements, swedes are actually larger, sweeter and generally hardier than turnips.

The swede is a superb winter root vegetable which stores for ages in cool climates without losing any of its mild nutty flavour. Its skin is not really edible but once peeled, swede is delicious boiled, steamed, mashed or grated raw into salads. One word of warning – do not overcook swede as its flavour will increase disastrously.

recipe

Stokehole Delight (Spicy Mashed Swedes) (see page 57)

Tomato

(Lycopersicon lycopersicum)

The enterprising Spaniards first introduced tomatoes collected from the South American Andes into Europe during the early sixteenth century. Becoming popular in Italy and France long before the English recognised their potential, tomatoes were known by the

French as 'love apples' and by the Italians as 'golden apples'. Initially grown in England as an ornament or curiosity and wrongly purported to be poisonous, they were not considered suitable for human consumption until the early 1800's.

During the last 200 years, no other vegetable (although it is technically a berry) has been exploited quite like the tomato with copious attention received from breeders, seed multinationals, home gardeners and the latest revival of interest in saving unusual non-hybrid heritage varieties from obscurity. The tomato is also one of the few vegetables where flavour is dictated equally by its variety and its freshness. Unfortunately today, commercial pressures and profitability have bred out much of the tomato's inherent sweetness leaving it up to the home and organic gardener to produce a diversity of deliciously juicy tomatoes as they should be. Discernible differences in sweetness and acidity as well as an array of colours, shapes and sizes make some tomatoes more suitable for particular cooking uses than others – for example, yellow or red cherry tomatoes are supremely sweet for salads while the marvellously tasty Italian roma varieties make excellent sauces and soups. An exhaustive number of dishes may include this wonderfully versatile vegetable, whether raw; peeled or not; cooked quickly or stewed for hours; baked, grilled or barbecued.

recipes

Cherry Tomatoes and Basil (see page 58)
Spicy Tomato Sauce (see page 74)

Turnip

(Brassica rapa)

Originally from Europe and northern Asia, turnips, similar to swede in appearance and growth requirements, have been long in cultivation but, unlike swede, will not store for long periods.

Turnips are most often peeled before cooking and the young, immature ones are surprisingly delicious as a raw salad vegetable. Whole roasted turnips in their jackets, *vis-à-vis* potatoes, are particularly delectable.

recipe

Turnip and Potato Soup (see page 17)

Heligan Fruit

(with recipe references)

Apple

(Malus pumila)

Commercially grown in vast quantities in every cool corner of the world today, the apple must be one of the first fruits ever cultivated. The large, sweet fruit of today has evolved over generations from the native small, sour crab apples of Europe. Even though thousands of named varieties exist today, typical of modern utilitarian motives, only a relatively few are available commercially. Infamous for its role in Adam and Eve's Fall, the Tree of the Knowledge of Good and Evil is generally believed to be the humble, unassuming apple. Highly popular in Victorian and Edwardian England, this versatile fruit was prepared in all sorts of ways, as illustrated in Georgiana Hill's household manual on *How to Cook Apples shown in A Hundred Different Ways*, written in 1867.

With the abundance of varieties available, comes a choice of flavours, colours, shapes and textures. Apples these days are usually separated into eating and cooking types – cooking ones have quite a tart flavour whilst eating apples are deliciously sweet. As witnessed by Mrs Hill, there are at least a hundred different uses for apples to suit every appetite, whether sweet or savoury.

recipes

Orchard Apple Tart (see page 76)
Apple Muffins (see page 77)
Kim's Gooseberry and Apple Pie (see page 88)
Miss Tremayne's Melon Cup (see page 93)
Annabel's Red Cabbage (see page 36)

Apricot

(Prunus armeniaca)

Of Chinese origin, apricots were cultivated for thousands of years before being introduced to sixteenth century English society by one of King Henry VIII's resourceful gardeners.

Most commercial varieties of apricot are destined for drying or other processed methods, such as apricot jam. You will find that dried apricots, rather than fresh, are so easily available all year round that they are often prescribed for modern recipes, performing equally well in sweet and savoury dishes. When using the dried forms, just be aware that the brightly coloured plump and fleshy types have been processed with the help of sulphur dioxide and dyes, whereas the brown, wrinkled ones are naturally sun-dried giving them a wonderfully different and exceptional flavour.

recipes

Ann's Apricot Flummerie (see page 78)
Apricots with Almond Filling (see page 79)

Banana

(Musa sp.)

No-one knows for certain where exactly bananas came from originally – although it is reasonable to assume they originate in warm tropical regions of the world where Chinese and South Asian records provide us with some clues.

Nowadays, the economic stability of certain countries like Honduras is based on the banana export industry, where worldwide demand can make or break them – just ask Woody Allen, whose film *Bananas* satirises the not-so-mythical 'banana republic'. Exported bananas are picked green for better transportability and storage life – this does not necessarily adversely affect their flavour or quality. It's a shame that inhabitants of cool regions can only sample one or two varieties of banana, due to the limited storage qualities of other exotic varieties. All bananas are extremely delicious in their pure unadulterated form, except for the variety plantain, which is tough and unpalatable until fried or baked.

recipes

Real Banana Milkshake (see page 81)
Jungle Banana Bread (see page 80)
Heligan Fruit Salad (see page 87)

Blackberry

(Rubus fruticosus)

Otherwise known as brambles, blackberries tend to run rampant if left unmanaged as many a gardener's shredded glove will testify. Raspberry, loganberry and boysenberry all belong to the blackberry's genus of Rubus which includes over 2000 varieties of blackberry – most of these are wild forms with only a very few commercially cultivated.

Contrary to common belief, raspberry and blackberry are not always differentiated by colour – some raspberries are actually black, while some blackberries are red. One way to tell the difference is by picking them – the whole blackberry with its centre will be pulled away, whereas the raspberry's centre will be left behind on the stem. Although cultivated blackberries are usually bigger and more luscious-looking than the wild forms, they are not necessarily more luscious-tasting, as often the wild ones are the sweetest. Nothing is better than eating a handful of fresh blackberries in the summer sun, while blackberry jams, sorbets and puddings with lashings of cream can be just as wonderful.

recipes

Blackberry Sauce (see page 81)
Blackberry and Raspberry Pudding (see page 82)

Currant, Red and White

(Ribes rubrum)

The red and white currants of today descend from wild European and Asian forms which can still be found. Red currants in particular, captured the imagination of fifteenth century Europe for their delicate beauty as well as their delicious berries.

Not usually eaten raw, both red and white currants make deliciously tart preserves, jams, pies and sauces. The separate species of blackcurrant *(R. nigrum)* was considered a rather inferior berry, snubbed by Victorian English society until the discovery of Vitamin C in the late nineteenth century raised its profile, bringing blackcurrants' medicinal value to the fore – but it wasn't until well into the 1900's that the blackcurrant was fully accepted into the culinary realm.

recipe

Red and White Currant Pie (see page 85)

Fig

(Ficus carica)

Originally from Mediterranean and Middle Eastern regions, the cultivated form of fig as we know it today dates back to pre-Pharaoh times, with its large decorative leaves gaining holy import through clothing the nakedness of Adam and Eve. Arriving in Britain and North America in the early sixteenth century, only three or four commercial varieties are grown today – these include common figs and the extra large golden brown Smyrna figs.

Fresh uncooked figs may be eaten whole, skin and all, and have a delightfully grainy texture, delicious with cream, yoghurt or cheese. Probably better known dried, they are used extensively in cakes, puddings and biscuits, as well as being a delectable nutritious snack for the sweet-toothed amongst us.

recipe

Figs and Berry Cream (see page 86)

Gooseberry

(Ribes reticulata)

Growing wild in cool, moist climates across the world, the gooseberry has been developed and exploited most extensively in Britain over the years. One of the first records of gooseberry cultivation in Britain appears in the early thirteenth century, with their popularity reaching a peak during the eighteenth and nineteenth centuries.

Picking gooseberries can be a painful experience for the uninitiated, but once the bush is trained into a goblet shape, avoiding the extremely sharp thorns is made easier. Not only green, but of various shades from yellow through to red, cultivated forms can be fairly sweet (especially the dessert gooseberry), but the wild ones are very bitter. You will find that gooseberries in general will need sweetening up to create delicious pies, sauces and sorbets.

recipes

Kim's Gooseberry and Apple Pie (see page 88)
Gooseberry Fool (see page 89)

Grape

(Vitis sp.)

Grapes are native to several parts of the world including the Mediterranean, parts of North America and some of southern Africa. Although these disparate species are still widely cultivated, the Mediterranean type, *Vitis vinifera* is now the most dominant grape throughout the globe comprising thousands of varieties – but only a select few are grown for the honoured tasks of winemaking and table use.

As the wine connoisseur will tell you, grape varieties come in different sizes; seeded or seedless; colours from pale green through to deep purple; and have markedly divergent flavours. Grape cultivation is not only big business for wine-makers, but dried fruit companies make good use of grapes in the form of raisins, currants and sultanas, according to variety. Freshly picked juicy sweet grapes, no longer the symbol of Roman decadence, are thankfully readily available to us all these days.

recipes

Lettuce Salad with Grapes and Cashews (see page 24)
Grapes with Orange Sauce (see page 89)
Heligan Fruit Salad (see page 87)

Lemon

(Citrus limon)

Lemons actually originally came from northern Asia, not the Mediterranean as most would suppose – an understandable misconception since lemons have been grown in the temperate Mediterranean for nearly two thousand years, since the first century. It is hard for us today to imagine what a life without lemons would be like, but it wasn't until the late 1400's that this essential fruit spread into Europe and North America.

Lemons are a wonderfully energy efficient food, producing little waste where the skin, juice and flesh all have multifarious uses. Just remember to wash the skin to remove pesticide residues (unless grown organically) – something we tend to forget about with lemons – then grate, peel, juice or slice them.

recipes

Lemon Meringue Pie (see page 90)
Lemon Mousse (see page 91)

Melon

(Cucumis melo)

The melon's ancestry most probably goes back to the warmer climes of the Near East and northern India. Many and varied melon varieties exist today after spreading through into the New World around the late 1400's. Requiring warm temperatures and specialised conditions, the melon was welcomed with great enthusiasm in Victorian England where glasshouse technology and ingenuity were at their zenith.

Some of the better known types include cantaloupe, winter and honeydew melons, all supremely sweet and refreshing. A good ripe melon needs no added sugar, only a touch of lemon juice or even some salt, pepper or ginger as an exotic alternative.

recipes

Melon with Coconut (see page 92)
Miss Tremayne's Melon Cup (see page 93)

Nectarine

(Prunus persica var. *nectarina)*

The true origins of the nectarine are yet to be discovered, but records show that European cultivation dates back to the sixteenth century. In actual fact a variety of peach, the nectarine is not a hybrid between plum and peach as most people are led to believe – an understandable mistake as the flavour is quite like a mixture between the two.

Usually picked when unripe, this fruit will store well and lose none of its delectable sweetness when ripened at home. Use them in the same way you would for peaches and plums, substituting for each other whenever you like.

recipes

Nectarines in Syrup (see page 93)
Nectarines in Brandy Cream (see page 94)
Heligan Fruit Salad (see page 87)

Orange

(Citrus sinensis)

Oranges originate in China where their rind was prized more for its fragrance than the flesh for its flavour. From there, oranges made their way westwards to Spain by the first century and then into Italy and Portugal by the fifteenth century.

Oranges of many different varieties are now cultivated in massive quantities throughout the world, in both hemispheres. For example, the extremely sweet navel developed in Brazil; valencias grown in the United States; jaffas from Israel and blood oranges of the Mediterranean. Not all oranges are meant to be sweet – the bitter Seville variety is highly valued for making marmalade and substituting for lemon juice in savoury dishes.

recipes

Baked Orangey Custard (see page 95)
Grapes with Orange Sauce (see page 89)
Summer Strawberries and Orange (see page 104)
Heligan Fruit Salad (see page 87)

Peach

(Prunus persica)

Of Chinese descent, the original wild peach was quite small and sour, very different from the large, juicy and sweet fruit of today. Its cultivation and evolution spread west across into Persia then the Mediterranean and eventually reached Britain and North America around the sixteenth century.

Only two distinct types exist today – clingstone and freestone, indicating how easily the flesh will separate from the large central stone. Traditional peaches and cream conjure an image of English country picnics in the summer sun but for a modern alternative, try them with yoghurt or even in a curry.

recipes

Gingered Peaches (see page 95)
Baked Peachy Custard (see page 96)

Pear

(Pyrus communis)

The sweet pears of today have evolved over thousands of years from the original wild species of central Europe and northern Asia, but it wasn't until the 1700's in Belgium that the first really soft, juicy pear was created. A favourite of Louis XIV in the 1600's, he encouraged serious cultivation practices and the development of diverse varieties, while simultaneously in North America, quite different varieties from seed were being bred.

Pears are so well-known to us that we all understand immediately what is meant by the description 'pear-shaped'. These days, however, this could be a bit of a misnomer as some varieties like the Asian pear, are actually spherical! Pears are usually picked unripe, allowing us (the consumer) to perfectly time the degree of ripeness precisely, according to our own taste. A helpful trick to prevent cut pears discolouring is to immediately dip the pieces into lemon juice.

recipes

Spicy Pears in Red Wine Syrup (see page 97)
Chocolate Pear Bake (see page 98)

Pineapple

(Ananas comosus)

Pineapples are still found wild in Brazil where the Portuguese and Spanish first discovered them during the great explorations of the fifteenth century. The first Spanish explorers called them *piña* due to their resemblance to a pine cone while their generic name comes from the local Brazilian word *anana*, meaning 'excellent fruit'. Pineapple cultivation in Europe and England has a fascinating and colourful history, being first grown during Charles II's reign in 1661 where they were greeted with much curiosity and attention. Victorian English horticulturists later perfected the hothouse 'pineapple pit' with heat generated via naturally composting manures. During those times, pineapples were thrust into the limelight, constantly used as decorative motifs on crockery through to building arches.

Only three or four main varieties exist today, including a very pretty miniature form. Big business for multinational corporations, most of the commercially grown pineapples are destined for the canning or drying industry, but the flavour is a far cry from the fragrant sweetness of a juicy freshly cut slice. A perfectly ripe fruit needs no company, but a slightly under-ripe one can be improved with a little honey or sugar.

recipes

Queen's Pineapple-Rum Bread Pudding (see page 99)
Winch's Chilled Pineapple Cake (see page 100)

Plum

(Prunus sp.)

The earliest plums were cultivated in China thousands of years ago with the first records of plums in England found in medieval monasteries – often the centre of horticultural experimentation of those times.

The many different types of plums today are divided into two basic groups – cooking and eating. Within these two groups, various species of diverse colours and flavours exist, such as the sweet greengage eating plum and the tart damson cooking variety.

recipes

Plum Pie Crumble (see page 101)
Heligan Fruit Salad (see page 87)

Raspberry

(Rubus ideaus)

First cultivated in ancient Greece, raspberries still grow wild in the cooler regions of the world, differing in colour and flavour from region to region – including unusual colours such as yellow, white, black and pale orange.

The difference between black raspberries and blackberries, both belonging to the same genus, is not only the flavour, but the central part of the raspberry remains on the bush when picked, whereas the blackberry's centre comes away with the fruit. Possessing a slightly tart flavour, fresh raspberries become even more delicious served with sugar or honey and cream, while cooked ones make superb syrups, cream purées, puddings and sorbets.

recipes

Samm's Raspberry Cream Pie (see page 102)
Blackberry and Raspberry Pudding (see page 82)

Rhubarb

(Rheum rhaponticum)

Although botanically speaking rhubarb is a stem or leaf vegetable, most people cook and eat it like a fruit so we have included it here along with the other fruits. Native to Siberia and the Himalayas, rhubarb was cultivated purely for medicinal purposes long before its wonderful culinary properties were discovered. Its first appearance in English recipe manuals was well into the 1700's, taking at least another hundred years to reach popular acceptance. Innovative Victorian English gardeners 'forced' rhubarb's growth into producing sweeter, tender stalks earlier than its normal season by covering them with clay pots, a practice in various guises still employed today.

Rhubarb is one of the few vegetables (or fruits!) whose stalks must unquestionably be cooked before consuming – its raw state is rather indigestible. Also be careful with the leaves – they should never be eaten in any way, shape or form as large amounts can be quite toxic to our digestive systems. Due to its innate tartness, rhubarb combines superbly well with inherently sweet fruit and berries, like strawberry.

recipes

Rhubarb Fuggle (see page 103)
Strawberry-Rhubarb Crumble (see page 105)

Strawberry

(Fragaria sp.)

Wild strawberries of every imaginable shape, colour and size exist in both hemispheres of the world today – ranging from red and pink through to yellow, white or green, some of which are at least five hundred years old. Most of the modern cultivated varieties are descendants from full-scale breeding programmes created by the enterprising Victorian English horticulturists.

Heralding the long-awaited summer, freshly picked succulent strawberries with whipped cream symbolise hot, lazy days in the countryside, and if you're lucky enough, a court-side seat at Wimbledon! The old adage, 'small is beautiful', well applies to cultivated strawberries – the smaller, the tastier, while wild species can have the best flavour of all. This delightful berry can be made into all sorts of sumptuous dishes such as mousse, ice-cream, cheesecake and biscuits, the list is endless.

recipes

Summer Strawberries and Orange (see page 104)
Strawberry-Rhubarb Crumble (see page 105)

Conversions

We have listed both British imperial and metric measurements in all recipes. These measurements are not exact conversions but are convenient equivalents to make life easier. Because of this, it is important not to alternate between metric and imperial measures in one recipe to avoid altering your results.

The following lists are some of the most common equivalent measures used in this book:

LIQUID MEASURES (VOLUME)

IMPERIAL		METRIC
	fluid ounces (fl.oz)	*millilitres (ml)*
	1	30
	3	90
	4	120
¼ pint	5	150
(1 cup)	8	240
½ pint	10	300
¾ pint	15	450
1 pint	20	600
1⅔ pint	33	1000 (1 litre)

SOLID MEASURES (WEIGHT)

IMPERIAL		METRIC
pounds (lb)	*ounces (oz)*	*grams (g)*
	½	15
	1	30
	2	60
¼	4	125
½	8	250
¾	12	375
1	16	500
2	32	1000 (1 kg)

OVEN TEMPERATURES

°F	°C	*gas mark*
300	150	2
325	170	3
350	180	4
375	190	5
400	200	6
425	220	7
450	230	8

SPOONS

¼ teaspoon		1.25ml
½ teaspoon		2.50ml
1 teaspoon		5.00ml
1 tablespoon	½ fl.oz.	15.00ml

About the Author:

Australian Deborah Stroh, a graduate horticulturist, has travelled the world following her twin passions for indigenous cooking and food cultivation.

About the Illustrator:

Zowie Keating, qualified teacher, specialises in highly detailed botanical illustrations in watercolour and pen-and-ink as well as miniature paintings. Her work is exhibited widely throughout Britain and she is President of the Cornish Fine Art Society. She was recently invited to illustrate rare orchids in Japan and now teaches painting to adult education learners in Cornwall, including regular classes at the Lost Gardens of Heligan.